Sidetracked

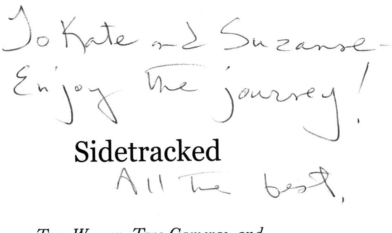

*To Kate and Suzanne—*
*Enjoy the journey!*

# Sidetracked

*All the best,*

*Two Women, Two Cameras, and*
*Lunches on Sherman's Trail*

*Jackie White*

## Milam McGraw Propst and
## Jaclyn Weldon White

MERCER UNIVERSITY PRESS | *Macon, Georgia*
2016

MUP/ P531

© 2016 by Mercer University Press
Published by Mercer University Press
1501 Mercer University Drive
Macon, Georgia 31207

9 8 7 6 5 4 3 2 1

Books published by Mercer University Press are printed
on acid-free paper that meets the requirements of the
American National Standard for Information Sciences—
Permanence of Paper for Printed Library Materials.


ISBN     978-0-88146-575-4
Cataloging-in-Publication Data is available from the
Library of Congress

For Kimberly White Ammons, who can do it all.
No matter what the obstacles, you accomplish
every goal you set with grace and love. You are an
inspiration, sweet girl.
—Jackie


Throughout the years of being an author, I've
dedicated books to my beloved family and
acknowledged several very special friends. Jackie
just called to remind me that it is dedication time
once again. A head-scratcher at first, the honoree
suddenly became obvious. Without her,
*Sidetracked* would never have come to be. I
dedicate our book to my talented co-author and
fellow traveler, Jaclyn Weldon White.
—Milam

# Contents

# Introduction

Milam Propst and Jackie White met at a book signing in 1999, only a few months after their first books were published by Mercer University Press. They were both new to the world of publishing, taking baby steps into the unknown, and soon discovered that those steps were easier to take together. They've been close friends ever since. Over the years, they worked together, traveled together and, of course, lunched together—frequently and well. It was only a matter of time before they wrote together.

The original idea for this book was Jackie's. She proposed to Milam that they visit obscure historical markers in Georgia as they followed Sherman's infamous route to the sea. They'd travel to the sites, make notes and, of course, stop for lunch—usually in a meat and three. For the uninitiated, that's a restaurant serving one meat—likely fried chicken—and three side orders of starch and overcooked southern vegetables, with cornbread or biscuits, and usually cobbler for dessert.

Milam was less than enthusiastic. She had little interest in history, especially the years of the Civil War, and wasn't sure she wanted to spend that much time traveling around the state of Georgia. But she didn't want to rush to judgment and Jackie had already started the research. One of the places she wanted to visit was a 180-year-old house in Dekalb County.

"It's the oldest house in the county and I just found out it was built by Carl's great-great-great-great grandfather!" Jackie said.

The mention of Jackie's late husband was all it took. Milam agreed to give the project a chance. All they had to do was map out their route and go.

It didn't turn out to be that simple. For starters, they discovered that Sherman split his army into two flanks, so there were actually *two* routes to the sea. Straight lines were out of the question. And neither Milam nor Jackie have a sense of direction good enough to navigate a one-traffic-light town. They'd once circled the city of Athens three times in search of a bookstore where they were scheduled for a signing.

They're also easily sidetracked. As a result, they got lost pretty often and made a bunch of U-turns, but they ended up with some wonderful stories to tell. And, of course, they had lots of lunches along the way.

# Sherman's Progress

## Fulton County

The United States entered its fourth year of civil war in 1864. General William Tecumseh Sherman and his troops moved steadily southward. By May they were beginning their campaign to take the city of Atlanta. Union forces massed north and southeast of the city. In early July, Sherman was headquartered in Sandy Springs and, on July 18, they moved into Buckhead.

# The Storyteller

## JWW

We started our adventure close to home in Fulton County. On a warm spring Tuesday morning, I met Milam at her Sandy Springs home and she drove us to nearby Buckhead. These days it's known for its upscale neighborhoods and trendy shops, but this affluent suburb in north Atlanta had humble beginnings.

A tavern was located here in the 1830s when the area was still mostly wilderness. The small settlement was originally known as Irbyville for the resident Irby family. But a hunter hung a deer's head on the front of the tavern where it remained for some time and became an identifying landmark. Soon the place became known as Buckhead.

It was a tranquil little place for decades. More settlers moved in and sections of the forests were replaced by farms. But that changed in July of 1864 when Sherman and his army massed in the area as they prepared to move on Atlanta.

Of course, the wilderness is long gone now and there was no sound of distant gunfire the morning we visited there. The streets of Buckhead were jammed with traffic and people rushed along the sidewalks past all sorts of shops and businesses. Unlike them, we weren't in a hurry. We had no business to conduct nor any shopping to do. We were there to visit Charlie Loudermilk Park and get a look at The Storyteller.

The only problem was parking. We circled the area, breaking for the occasional jaywalker, for what seemed like a long time until a metered spot opened up just opposite the park. Milam quickly pulled into it.

Scrounging in our purses, we came up with six quarters between us. We shoved them one by one into the meter, but it didn't respond. An ominous little sign behind the glass read "dead."

"Is it broken?" I asked.

"I think it wants more money," Milam said.

But we'd exhausted our supply of change. In other circumstances, we'd probably have just taken our chances, but the city of Atlanta had recently gained notoriety for excessive parking enforcement. We didn't want to invite a ticket by leaving the car next to a nonfunctioning (or underpaid) meter. So I grabbed the camera, hopped out, and ran across the street to get a few pictures of The Storyteller while Milam circled Buckhead's convoluted blocks.

Dominating the center of the little urban park, The Storyteller is a sculpture by Frank Fleming—a large, seated masculine figure with a deer's head, complete with enormous antlers. Gathered around him are the figures of several dogs and a rabbit, all listening to him telling the story of how Buckhead got its name.

In my research I'd learned that over in Birmingham there's a similar piece by the same artist, except that it has a fountain, more woodland animals, and the storytelling creature has a ram's head rather than a buck's. It also has had more than its share of controversy.

Shortly after it was installed, the Alabama sculpture caused a stir. Accusations of devil worship and paganism flew around it for some time, evidently the result of the ram's head. Fortunately our Georgia Storyteller is just a charming statue with a benign expression.

I hurried to snap a few pictures and, in less than five minutes, was dashing back across the busy street where Milam picked me up. She pulled out into traffic and we were on our way, complaining about thieving parking meters.

"Did you get the pictures?" she asked.

I was reviewing them on the screen of the camera. "Yeah, they look okay." I laughed. "He's a very handsome statue. You should have seen him close up. I wish I could have had my picture taken sitting on his lap."

That was all the encouragement Milam needed. She whipped into a parking lot, quickly negotiated a path through the cars, made a sharp turn, and we were back on Peachtree Street, heading into the heart of Buckhead once again.

There was still no place to park, but Milam had grown bolder. She pulled into the lot of the Bank of America located next to the park and stopped the car at the curb. A security guard—tall, serious, and dressed in black military-looking clothes—started toward us.

"Could we please park here for just a minute?" Milam asked, giving him her sweetest smile. She breathlessly explained what we were doing and why we wanted to visit the little park. The guard was charmed by her, just as most people are, and gave us permission to leave the car there.

Back in Loudermilk Park I got my wish. I sat on The Storyteller's hard metal lap while Milam took pictures.[1] Unfortunately the picture didn't turn out as I hoped. We used another for this book and I'll keep the one of The Storyteller and me just for myself.

Back at the bank, the guard was waiting for us. We learned his name was Eddie Sharpe "with an e" and that, although he'd worked there for years, he'd never actually set foot in the park next door. But our description of the sculpture must have interested him at least a little.

"At lunch," he said, "I'm going over there and have a look at it."

I was smiling as we left Buckhead. Not only did we visit The Storyteller, but we just might have introduced Eddie Sharpe to a little bit of local history.

---

[1] Since our visit, Loudermilk Park has redesigned and The Storyteller has been removed. We hope he shows up somewhere else very soon.

The Storyteller

# Roswell Factory and the Old Bricks

## JWW

After my close encounter with The Storyteller, we drove ten miles north to Roswell. A mill town during its early existence and now one of Atlanta's numerous suburbs, it has a colorful, but tragic history. The small downtown is packed with interesting shops, theaters, restaurants, and museums, and it boasts several stately homes, including Barrington Hall and Bulloch Hall.

We drove down Bulloch Avenue and saw Bulloch Hall, beautiful and serene in the afternoon sun. It was quite a contrast to how it must have looked when the town was occupied by Federal troops in July of 1864 and the Hall and many other homes in town were used as barracks and officers' quarters for the invading army.

I'd like to say that our thoughts were fixed on historic import and cultural enrichment as we drove into Roswell that afternoon, but I can't. We were focused firmly on our stomachs. It was past 1:00 and Milam declared she was starving.

"We have to have lunch," she said, "before we do anything else."

I didn't argue.

We chose the Roswell Public House on South Atlanta Street for no reason other than it was there and it was open. Located on the ground floor of an 1854 building, it has been a shop, a hospital, a funeral home, and now a restaurant.

And what would an old building be without ghosts? While we ate some truly delicious food, our server Sarah told us about Catherine and Michael, two star-crossed lovers who died here during the Civil War and are said to still haunt the place. She told us that people say they've heard a piano playing from the second floor, and thumps that were thought to be Catherine and Michael dancing to the music.

"Have you ever heard that?" Milam asked.

"No. I don't believe in spirits."

"So you've never had any strange experiences here?"

"Well ..."

She admitted that weird things had happened when she was closing the restaurant. She explained that the front door is equipped with a bell that rings whenever it's opened and closed. A few times, Sarah said, she'd heard the bell and hurried out of the back of the restaurant only to find that no one was there. And a couple of times she'd heard children's voices, but no children were anywhere around. Still, she wouldn't go so far as to say she thought these things had anything to do with ghosts.

After lunch, we set off to find the ruins of Roswell Mill. We followed signs along a quiet side street and then down a very steep concrete walk to a tree-shaded spot where a modern covered bridge spans the Chattahoochee River. This idyllic place, once the location of the mill, was the site of a tragedy more than 150 years ago.

Roswell was a thriving textile center in the mid-1800s. It was here during the Civil War that the woolen cloth known as confederate gray and used for army uniforms, was produced. That fact made the Roswell Mill a prime target for the Union Army. Federal troops burned it and several other mills in the area to the ground.

That destruction wasn't enough for the conquering army. General Sherman ordered that the nearly four hundred mill workers, most of whom were women and children, be charged with treason, even though the only crime these poor people committed was trying to earn a living.

As punishment, they and their dependents were rounded up and held in the Roswell town square for several days, sleeping out in the open, until they could be loaded into railroad cars. They were given nine days' food rations and shipped north to Indiana. While a very few made their way back to Roswell after the war, the fate of most of them is unknown. Georgia author Frances Patton Statham fictionalized the sad story in her novel *The Roswell Women*.

The walk back up the hill wasn't the easiest thing we'd ever done—kind of like climbing a short Stone Mountain—but seeing the mill site had been worth it. And a cool April breeze kept us from overheating.

Before leaving Roswell, we took a walk down Sloan Street. Here we found The Old Bricks. The two small two-story buildings look like the luxury townhouses that they now are. However, in 1839, they were built as housing for the mill workers and, in 1864, served as a hospital for Union soldiers.

As we stood looking at the sedate gray buildings, I wondered how often today's residents reflected on the history all around them.

Old Roswell Mill

# Williams-Payne House

## MMP

Jackie White and I have been friends for years, but when she asked me to write a travel book with her, a book that required doing research, I refused. I adamantly refused.

"Working together could destroy our friendship. I care about that," I insisted. "Besides, I can't stand research."

"I'd do that part," she countered. "We'll have fun."

The discussion continued for months.

"Jackie, how many times do I have to say it? NO!"

"Yes," she purred.

"No," I snarled.

A lunch or two later, the subject of co-authoring a book resurfaced.

"Again," Jackie pressed me, "why not?"

"Well, okay, maybe I'd contribute a story or two."

For my initial effort, I wanted to impress Jackie, so I played my ace card and called in a big dog. Some refer to Garnett Cobb as the *Queen of Sandy Springs*.

A lady I know once remarked, "When I grow up, I want to BE Garnett Cobb."

Garnett is my friend; actually, we like to think of each other as family. Her niece, Betty Ann Putnam Colley, is one of my oldest friends. The following story may be about the Williams-Payne House Museum, but it's really my tribute to Garnett. A wife and mother, retired banker, and community activist extraordinaire, she was involved with the Sandy Springs community well past her hundredth birthday. Much to her credit, she also rescued a historic home and moved it to its current location.

Here's the story.

Like so many of Atlanta's historic landmarks, the Williams-Payne House, circa: 1869, was headed for certain demolition. In the summer of 1984, it stood in the direct path of GA 400. Fortunately, Garnett, president of Sandy Springs Garden Club, would rally her troops.

I couldn't wait to show off Garnett to Jackie. She and I walked into Mount Vernon Towers and took the elevator up to Garnett's fifth floor apartment. As always, my friend was beautifully dressed, this day in lime green. Garnett greeted us with her signature grin and invited us to sit down. Several inches short of five feet tall and pushing one hundred and two years old, she amazed Jackie with her sharp mind.

"So Garnett, tell us how the Williams-Payne House Museum came to be."

"One summer morning, I woke up with a brainstorm," she beamed. "I'd been worried about my fellow club member, Marie Payne, and what had become of her cherished home of forty-two years.

"Sadly, after Marie moved out, it crumbled into disrepair. Homeless people had trashed it. I contacted the owners, Portman-Barry Investors, and discovered a couple of potential owners were planning to move the structure." Her big brown eyes twinkled. "Imagine relocating an entire house!

"Just as quickly, I decided we ladies of the Sandy Springs Garden Club could move Marie's house ourselves! What better use for her home than to become a meeting place for us and for others?"

Relying on her years in banking, Garnett convinced Portman-Barry to donate Marie's cottage to her garden club. She then phoned Frances Glenn Mayson and her husband Joey, both of whom were already active in the community. Five years of their own loving renovation of the magnificent Glenridge Hall (1929) should have convinced the young couple to pass on the idea. However, with a confident smile, she remembered Frannie's enthusiastic response, "Yes, of course, Garnett. Joey and I are IN!"

Businesses throughout Sandy Springs quickly jumped onto Garnett's bandwagon. Marie Payne's house would, indeed, be moved from its original location on Mount Vernon Highway to 6075 Sandy Springs Circle.*

On October 9, 1985, the roof of Payne's home was collapsed. Like the launching of a new battleship, the house, then secured on the back of a flatbed truck, was christened with a bottle of champagne. It was carefully and slowly moved one and a half miles down Hammond Drive to Sandy Springs Circle. Among those on the ride were Garnett and John Cobb and his sister, Frances Cobb Putnam, Betty Ann's mother.

"We celebrated afterwards with breakfast at the International House of Pancakes," recalled Garnett.

During restoration, architect Lane Greene discovered heart pine flooring throughout the structure. Garnett explained with a chuckle that Marie's lovely floors had been long protected by the more stylish "wall-to-wall carpeting." As the Paynes' modern additions were removed, the original structure was slowly revealed. The 1940s home concealed the residence of Jerome and Harriet Williams, a gem, a prime example of a nineteenth century country cottage.

Garnett turned one hundred years old on October 3, 2009. Her children, Tommy and Sandra Cobb, hosted a party at the Williams-Payne House. Attending were two hundred and fifty of Garnett's closest friends. She always regretted not being able to invite everyone she wanted due to the lack of space!

Sandy Springs Mayor Eva Galambos honored her with a proclamation from the city of Sandy Springs, while Joey Mayson saluted the guest of honor by announcing the terrace level of the Williams-Payne house would be named The Garnett Cobb Garden Room. These were but two of the many honors for a retired lady, who awakened one summer morning with a brainstorm.

On a personal note, I've had the honor of speaking at a couple of meetings in the Garnett Cobb Garden Room. My own group, the Westfield Garden Club, has also hosted a gathering at the Williams-Payne House Museum. Often, when I'm on the property, I can feel Garnett's presence.

Sadly, my friend passed away in October of 2013, four days after we celebrated her one hundred and fourth birthday at The Brickery in Sandy Springs.

I hope Garnett would be pleased with this story. I know she would insist upon my writing the book with Jackie. They'd connected nicely with each other.

"Okay, Jackie, Garnett, I'll do it."

---

*Beginning in the mid 1840s, Sandy Springs Campground became a summer gathering place for church services and fellowship. Participants numbered into the thousands. Originally called Oak Grove, the community would be designated Sandy Springs because of the clear, bubbling waters from a nearby natural spring. The spring is now a focal point on the grounds of the Williams-Payne House Museum.

Williams-Payne House

# Rhodes Hall

## MMP

Jackie gasped as we walked toward Rhodes Hall, Atlanta's Castle on Peachtree.

"It's gorgeous!" she said, stepping back to capture the perfect picture.

Our praises continued as we toured the lavish eighteenth century home, which was built from 1902 to 1904. Amos Giles Rhodes, founder of Rhodes Furniture was one of Atlanta's most successful entrepreneurs during the late 1800s. His Romanesque Revival style mansion was constructed from Stone Mountain granite. Designed as a place in which he'd retire and entertain, Le Reve (The Dream), currently showcases some of his original furnishings and personal items. It is open to the public for tours, weddings, and family celebrations.

"As you can see, this home was designed for entertaining," said Nawana Wilkerson, membership manager for the Georgia Trust for Historic Preservation, which is headquartered in the mansion. As she spoke, she was standing at the base of the magnificent circular staircase, which is enhanced by stunning stained glass windows memorializing the Confederacy.

My husband Jamey and I have attended several beautiful parties in Rhodes Hall, so we can attest to Nawana's comment about it being the perfect venue for parties. During one wedding reception, Jamey excused himself from the festivities and made his way toward the elegant stairway.

"Jamey Propst, you are not allowed up there!" I warned.

Just as quickly, a watchful lady stopped him in his tracks. "Sorry, sir, but upstairs is off limits."

Apparently, this wasn't the first time she'd halted a curious guest, especially after the television reality show *Ghost Hunters* conducted an investigation here. Were the spirits of the Rhodes family welcoming to the paranormal investigators as they crept about throughout Atlanta's famous stone castle?

I shared my embarrassing incident with Nawana.

"I'm afraid your husband was a little off track," she snickered. "All of our ghosts are in the basement!"

I couldn't wait to tell Jamey and did so as soon as I got home.

"I remembered that from *Ghost Hunters*," he said with a cocky turn of his head. "When you and that woman weren't looking," he admitted, "I sneaked down to the basement."

"And?"

"Nothing, I was pretty disappointed. So I came upstairs and ate a piece of wedding cake."

Was too much noise coming from the band? Had the ghosts of Rhodes Hall retreated from the wedding's commotion by hiding out of sight on the sleeping porch? Or maybe, just maybe, were they enjoying the party from the top of the stairs? After all, everyone talks about the businessman and his love of entertaining. Wouldn't festive music have played a big part in Amos Rhodes's original plan?

Rhodes Hall, Atlanta

# Searching for Early Atlanta

## JWW

Milam drove us to midtown Atlanta while I tried to tell her where to go next. My directions were sketchy at best since it had been over twenty years since I'd lived and worked in this area of town. But we eventually found our way to Piedmont Park, 189 beautiful, green acres in the middle of the city.

According to the marker we found there, this was the location of the 1895 Cotton States Exposition. During the one-hundred-day event, the park hosted a college football game, Buffalo Bill's Wild West Show, a visit by President Grover Cleveland, and the debut of a moving picture.

Of course, all that was way before our time. My memories of the place go back to the late 60s and early 70s when Piedmont Park served as a big backyard for the hippies and flower children who lived in the 15th Street area. I'd been there when bands like the Allman Brothers put on free concerts in the park and we were all excited by the advent of southern rock. You could get high just standing downwind of the crowd.

Today runners and bikers flock to the park. It's often crowded with families and is the site for festivals, concerts, and outdoor movies. Even though the morning we visited was overcast, it was warm. Joggers were racking up miles and dogs were being walked. A leisurely stroll by the lake would have been a nice diversion at another time, but today we had other places to see.

Following my halting directions, Milam drove us to West Peachtree Street. I was eager to show her another marker and another place where I'd spent a lot of time in my younger days.

Baltimore Block had been another center for the counterculture. The block of row houses, built in 1885 by Jacob Rosenthal, was Atlanta's first apartment development. An elegant address in its heyday, it eventually fell into disrepair. Then in the 1930s it was renovated into smaller apartments and began attracting artists, writers, and musicians.

In the 1960s a coffee shop and a bar called the Bottom of the Barrel moved in. Live music and long hair were the order of the day. I'd visited the Block and the bar several times and was looking forward to seeing it again.

"It's such a cool place," I told Milam as I directed her through the maze of midtown streets. "Looks like something from one of the cities up north. You'll love it."

When she turned off Spring Street onto Baltimore Place, Milam pulled to the curb. She looked around, confused.

"Are you sure this is the place?"

"Yes, at least it *should* be."

I was having trouble orienting myself to our location. The Block was there, I could see the row houses lining the street just ahead, but now they were only a tiny wing of a multi-floored office building. Instead of a quaint, quirky neighborhood, the street now looked like just about every other one in downtown Atlanta—shiny, new, and anonymous. There was even a guard shack between the block and us where we'd have to prove that we had business there before we could enter the property.

"It *was* the place," I said, disappointed. "It's not anymore. Let's go find Thrasherville."

Atlanta traces its beginning back to 1839 when John Thrasher built some rough shelters for laborers who would soon be working on a junction of two major railroads. Naturally, people began calling it Thrasherville. This was where a lot of Atlanta firsts happened: first baby was born, first church service held, first store opened, and, as is often the case with civic projects, the first labor disputes erupted.

We wanted to see the marker commemorating where all those firsts occurred, but we learned you have to be very quick. The marker is located on Marietta Street, right in front of the State Bar of Georgia. Milam steered through the heavy lunchtime traffic, braking frequently when other cars veered into our space, while I watched for the marker. I scanned the sidewalks jammed with pedestrians.

"There it is!" I said as we approached the Spring Street intersection, but Milam couldn't even give it a glance. She stopped at the light. I opened the door, snapped a picture over the car roof and got back in. The light changed and we were off again.

"Do you want to go back so you can see it, too?" I asked.

She swerved to avoid a medical services van that suddenly lurched away from the curb into our lane. "Don't think so," she said. Like me, I think she was just eager to get out of the congested area.

"Then just keep straight on Marietta Street."

We passed Centennial Olympic Park on our right. I told Milam that Carl and I spent an evening there during the '96 games. Carlos Santana was performing in the park and we danced to the music along with hundreds of other people. Everyone was having such a good time. Of course, that was several days before the bombing temporarily erased much of the high spirits and the city's sense of security.

A few miles out of town, Marietta Street crossed Northside Drive. On the northeast corner stood a historic marker, the only sign of the location where, on September 2, 1864, Atlanta mayor James Calhoun surrendered the city to Colonel John Coburn. In return, Calhoun asked only for the safety of the citizens. We learned later just how much his request meant to the Federal forces.

Atlanta may have begun at Thrasherville, but it certainly wasn't the first recorded settlement in this area. So we continued northwest to find the site of Standing Peach Tree, an eighteenth century Creek village that was located where Peachtree Creek joins the Chattahoochee River. Later, during the War of 1812, a fort of the same name was constructed close by. From the directions I'd found online, it seemed like a pretty straight shot. It wasn't.

We took turn after turn, trying to find our way. We saw industrial areas and neighborhoods and shopping centers. What we didn't see was Standing Peachtree. Even the GPS on my phone didn't help much—just kept leading us to dead ends and declaring that we were in "unverified" territory.

"Try that street to the right," I offered helpfully.

"Do you know for sure it's down there or are you just guessing?" Milam asked. I thought she sounded a little testy and didn't blame her. We'd already retraced our route several times.

Finally hunger overcame our interest in finding the sites and we stopped for a late lunch at Figo on Howell Mill Road. It was the best decision we'd made all day. We took our time with the meal. The pasta was delicious and the restaurant relaxing. We weren't only in better moods when we left, but the food evidently had a positive effect on our navigational abilities.

This time we found both locations with no problem. Of course, neither place bears any resemblance to the wild territory it once was. The site of the fort is now the property of the Atlanta Waterworks and the plaque for Standing Peach Tree is in an up-scale neighborhood built near the river. Still, if you put your mind to it, you can almost imagine hunters returning with their bounty, women cooking over open fires, and the fort clinging to the riverbank.

However, once we read the inscriptions on the markers, we experienced a major surprise. Everyone in Atlanta knows about the proliferation of Peachtrees. We have Peachtree Street, Peachtree Road, Peachtree Circle, Peachtree Industrial Avenue, etc., etc., etc. The best guess we've come up with is there are somewhere between fifty and one hundred streets in the Atlanta area with the word peachtree in them. This afternoon we learned that they were all misnamed.

Historians believe that the Creek village wasn't Standing Peach Tree. It was Standing *Pitch* Tree, meaning a pine tree from which tar, or pitch, could be obtained. The misunderstanding probably began when Governor John Martin wrote a letter to General Andrew Pickens in 1782 and mistakenly referred to a skirmish at the Standing *Peach* Tree settlement.

We've all heard jokes about no one ever seeing a peach tree on Peachtree Street. Well, now we know why. Peach trees may not be prolific in Atlanta, but you can certainly find plenty of pine trees.

THRASHERVILLE
Where Atlanta Began

In 1839 "Cousin John" Thrasher built a settlement called Thrasherville
at this then forested site near the peg marking the planned terminus
of the Western & Atlantic RR. This railroad was later built by the
State of Georgia to provide a link to the north for other Georgia
railroads. While building northward near Griffin, the Monroe RR
accepted John Thrasher's bid to build an embankment to enable a
future junction of the Monroe RR with the W&A RR. The Monroe
Embankment, a $25,000 project, required about two years to
complete. To fulfill his contract John Thrasher brought in many
laborers, built rough shelters to house them and opened Atlanta's
first store. Atlanta's first religious service, labor trouble, social
event and baby are associated with this settlement. In 1842 the
terminus was changed to the place now marked by the Zero Mile
Post, Thrasherville, Terminus and Marthasville were the names
given to the railroad generated settlement activity which preceded
Atlanta. Thrasherville and Terminus were unofficial names. Marthasville
was incorporated in 1843 and was reincorporated as Atlanta in 1845
and 1847. "Cousin John's" settlement at this location is where
Atlanta began.

GEORGIA HISTORICAL MARKER

Thrasherville marker

# The Martin Luther King, Jr.
## National Historic Site and the King Center

## JWW

Our next excursion was an inspirational one. The Martin Luther King, Jr. National Historic Site is on Auburn Avenue, just east of downtown Atlanta. Maintained and operated by the National Park Service, it memorializes the life, teachings, and accomplishments of Dr. King.

This wasn't Milam's first visit. "I brought several students from Germany here, oh, it must have been over twenty years ago. They were so impressed."

Here we found the house where he was born and lived for the first twelve years of his life. Nearby were historic Ebenezer Baptist Church, Freedom Hall, the Visitors Center, and the gravesites of Martin Luther King, Jr. and Coretta Scott King. Between the church and the tomb is The King Center for Nonviolent Social Change. Coretta Scott King established it after her husband's death. This is where we found the King Library and Archives.

During our time here, we saw exhibits highlighting Dr. King, Mrs. King, and Gandhi. It was Gandhi's nonviolent philosophy that shaped Dr. King's approach to the civil rights struggle.

We were standing beside the reflecting pool near the graves. Both of us had fallen silent, lost in our own thoughts. You can't be in a place like that and not grow pensive.

"I remember when I heard Dr. King had been assassinated in Memphis in 1968," I said. "I was in my apartment in Atlanta and, for a little while, I had trouble even absorbing the news. We'd only just started healing from President Kennedy's death. Then Martin Luther King was killed. How could something like that happen in our country? I felt like the world had turned upside down."

Milam gave me a sad smile. "My world had already turned up-side down. Jamey was in Vietnam, having left a few weeks after our wedding. When I heard about Dr. King," she shook her head, "it was like the country was being torn apart."

Atlanta has always been prominent in the civil rights move-ment, producing many of the key leaders and organizations. The Carter Center on nearby Freedom Parkway, which was founded in 1982 by President Jimmy Carter and Rosalynn Carter, works for human rights all over the world. And in 2014, the National Center for Civil and Human Rights Museum was opened here on Ivan Allen Boulevard. But after our time on Auburn Avenue that day, I think we both felt that the King Historic Site is the heart of that movement.

Entrance marker to the King Center

Tomb of Dr. Martin Luther King, Jr. and Coretta Scott King

# Ormewood, Grant Park, and Oakland

## MMP

"Oh shoot," lamented Jackie as we exited her car in front of Burns Cottage. "I meant to bring along a Robert Burns' poem to read aloud."

Too bad. That would have been most appropriate given our location. We were looking at the world's only exact replica of the Scottish cottage in which Robert Burns, the renowned poet and lyricist, was born.

Erected in 1910 by The Burns Club of Atlanta, the Burns Cottage on Alloway Place in Ormewood Park is still the site for the club's monthly meetings and for its annual celebration honoring Robert Burns (1759-1796). Not only was Burns well known as the National Poet of Scotland, but he is also regarded as the Poet Laureate of Freemasonry. A plaque on the outside wall of the cottage honors his membership in the ancient organization.

No well-spoken poem, only a snapshot taken, Jackie and I returned to her car and drove south on Confederate Avenue.

"I took my driver's test right there when I was sixteen," Jackie exclaimed as we passed the Georgia Department of Public Safety.

"So did I!"

We compared memories of those terrifying tests several decades ago only to discover we shared something else in common. Jackie and I barely squeaked by, because neither of us could parallel park. We each passed with the embarrassing grade of seventy percent, the minimum.

"A good solid C," I insisted.

Thus far in our quest to track down historical markers, we've never once had to park parallel, even if it meant we walked an extra block or two. Admittedly, my own lack of expertise with driving, especially in the area of navigation, has become all the more evident. Jackie admits she's not much better. We frequently make U-turns. We drive in multiple circles. On occasion, we've briefly headed the wrong way down a one-way street. I like to consider us consistent.

We drove through Ormewood Park and into Grant Park passing by the Atlanta Zoo and Cyclorama. When my son Jay was six, I took him to see the Cyclorama. When he spotted the flag of the United States, he jumped up and shouted, "It's going to be okay, Mommy! Here come the Americans!"

According to the news, the Cyclorama is being relocated to the Atlanta History Center, where it will undergo an extensive restoration. I plan to take our grandsons, Jay's nephews, Loftin and Emmett, to see the finished project. I may need to prepare an appropriate reply, should the comment about the American flag again arise.

Jackie and I ohhhed and ahhhed as we admired the area's charming historic homes, many redone, many painted in vivid Victorian colors, which enhance the remarkable architectural features of a century past. Even so, we found some of the people we encountered along the way to be equally intriguing.

"Look at that man!"

Eight feet from our car jogged a gentleman with an impeccably trimmed white beard and matching mane of hair. He sported a silk shirt and gym shorts. Looking for all the world like a latter day General Robert E. Lee, he proudly carried an enormous Confederate flag as he ran. No one else seemed to find him remarkable.

His one-man parade would have been even more exciting *if* Grant Park had been named for Ulysses S. Grant, admired by some as the victorious Civil War general. However, Grant Park was named for Lemuel Pratt Grant, a prominent Atlanta businessman, civic leader, and major landowner. In 1843, Grant, the father of four, donated one hundred acres of his own property for Atlanta's first park. He wanted to make certain that all children would have a nice place in which to play. Grant's 1856 mansion on St. Paul Avenue is one of only four remaining antebellum houses located within the current city limits of Atlanta.

It is apparent Lemuel Grant and Ulysses Grant had opposing plans for our fine city. Some of us are still mighty angry with the Yankee general.

While searching for a place to have lunch, we noticed another gentleman. This one, clean-shaven with blond hair and a receding hairline, was dressed in a jacket and slacks. He stood on a large boulder in the center of a small city park brimming with colorful wildflowers.

We circled back around a second time to be sure of what we were seeing. Yes, the man, facing historic Oakland Cemetery, was reading aloud from his Bible. Perhaps, the cemetery's residents couldn't hear his words, but Jackie and I admired his commitment to his peaceful congregation.

Founded in 1850, Oakland is a forty-eight-acre Victorian cemetery, but is far more than that. It is a lovely city park which hosts a plethora of events including family picnics, guided tours, an annual street festival, a fun run, and a festive gathering called Malts and Vaults. The only time the cemetery is open after dark is for Capture the Spirit, a gala Halloween celebration. Details for these and other events can be found on Oakland's website.

Enthralled, Jackie and I wandered among the some seventy thousand graves reading first one familiar name then another. As though we were turning the pages of an antique Atlanta telephone directory, I felt as if Jackie and I were tipping our hats both to Atlanta's finest along with those long forgotten.

Naturally, we visited the final resting place of Margaret Mitchell to pay our respects to the world famous author of *Gone with the Wind*. Oddly for us, we didn't have a moment's trouble finding her. With my husband in mind, we also sought out the world champion golfer, Bobby Jones (1902-1971). Jamey assures me that Jones was the best amateur player of all time. As is the custom, I added a golf ball to the pile of others on his grave.

We eventually wandered back to the car. The preacher man, taking no notice of our curiosity, was still there, reading his Bible to the faithful dead.

Burns Cottage

Oakland Cemetery

# The Margaret Mitchell House

## MMP

Because Jackie and I are writing a travel book following Sherman's March to the Sea, what more perfect historic site should we include than the place where Margaret Mitchell wrote her epic Civil War saga, *Gone with the Wind*?

Built in 1899 by Cornelius Sheehan, the Margaret Mitchell House started out as a stately three-story Tudor on Peachtree Street. In 1919, the elegant home was carved up into apartments. In 1925, Margaret (Peggy) and her husband John Marsh moved into apartment #1. She jokingly referred to their tiny quarters in the basement of the former mansion as The Dump.

Almost as if it were cursed, the building spiraled downward until 1978 when it was boarded up and left to rot. Seven years later, the community began efforts to save the important property. A tremendous challenge financially, the structure burned not once but twice. Even so, like Mitchell's feisty heroine Scarlett O'Hara, supporters rallied again and again. The house was named a city landmark in 1989 and finally opened to the public in May 1997.

Currently operated by the Atlanta History Center, the stately home was completely restored under the leadership of the house and museum's founder, Mary Rose Taylor. Today the Marshes' quarters, along with many of their personal items and furnishings, are carefully preserved in apartment #1 located on the back left side of the mansion.

Visitors can stand in the same window where Mitchell sat typing her Pulitzer-Prize winning novel. As did she, they might pretend to wave to her co-workers from the *Atlanta Constitution* as they rode by on the trolley.

"Hello, Peggy." One would ask kindly, "How's your ankle healing?"

Another would tease, "Are you writing the great American novel?"

Margaret Mitchell was doing just that. Her story about Scarlett O'Hara and Rhett Butler was to become one of the most successful books of all time. The 1939 film *Gone with the Wind*, which premiered in Atlanta's Loew's Grand Theatre, won ten Oscars, including the Academy Award for Best Motion Picture.

Dr. Otis W. Smith, the first African-American board certified pediatrician to practice in Georgia, had much to do with raising funds to rescue the Margaret Mitchell House. Toward the end of his medical career, Dr. Smith discovered his schooling at Meharry Medical College had been totally funded by the late Margaret Mitchell. He also found out the same was true for numerous others of his fellow graduates from Morehouse College.

The prominent physician yearned to do something to demonstrate his gratitude toward the benefactor he calls "Miss Mitchell." Dr. Smith and his wife joined a delegation headed by Mrs. Taylor to Daimler-Benz in Germany. As a result, the corporation donated more than five million dollars to restore the property. Today, an educational tourist attraction, the home and museum not only host visitors, but also offer unique literary and social events for the entire community.

Many years ago, I was honored to interview Dr. Smith for a magazine article about his role is saving the historic site. I was chatting with the charming gentleman and taking his picture when, on impulse, I shared my own aspirations with him.

"I'm writing a book," I began.

Dr. Smith encouraged me and suggested I stand near the window where the old trolley used to pass by. He insisted on taking my picture saying, "I hope this brings you luck with your novel."

I still have the photo. Dr. Smith's gesture, along with the spirit of the great Southern author, may have worked for my benefit. My first book was published in 1999.

Thank you, Dr. Smith.

While on a tour of the Margaret Mitchell House, one in our group inquired about the portrait of Sister Mary Melanie. The Catholic nun, the former Mattie Holliday, was a beloved cousin and frequent companion of Margaret Mitchell. The gentle nun served as the inspiration for the character of Melanie in *Gone with the Wind*.

Next to her portrait was that of a gentleman, John Holliday, another of Margaret Mitchell's cousins, a cousin by marriage. It was rumored that the Holliday cousins, Mattie and John, may once have been romantically linked. A match between cousins, even if "by marriage," would have been absolutely forbidden in those days.

John became the character of Ashley Wilkes in *Gone with the Wind*. As those of us who cherish this story well remember, Ashley married the sweet Melanie. Our guide let us in on a secret. In real life, John Holliday was lured to the West, where he became the notorious Doc Holliday!

Sister Mary Melanie lived in the convent for the remainder of her life and worked as a nurse at St. Joseph's Hospital in Atlanta. Most assuredly, part of me honors religious vocations. However, Margaret Mitchell's giving Ashley his Melanie makes me smile.

Jackie agrees.

# Sherman's Progress

## DeKalb County

Federal troops moved out from Roswell on July 18, 1864. Their goal was Stone Mountain where they would cut off rail service to Atlanta and isolate the city. They met resistance near what is now Briarcliff Road, but overcame it. Sherman set up his headquarters on Clairmont Road. Some of the troops camped near Nancy's Creek while others marched on the town of Decatur.

# Solomon Goodwin's Residence

## JWW

When doing some initial research for this book, I made a list of historic markers I thought we might want to visit and came across one for the Solomon Goodwin house—the oldest extant house in DeKalb County. It seemed interesting enough to include in our itinerary. Although it wasn't open to the public, we could, at least, stop by for a look at a structure that had been standing for more than 180 years.

At the time, the name sounded vaguely familiar, but it was several days before I realized why it was nagging me. I pulled out my old genealogy files and there it was. Solomon Goodwin was my late husband Carl's great-great-great-great grandfather! Now I was *really* interested.

It was about eleven that Friday morning when we found the Solomon Goodwin marker standing on the shoulder of busy Peachtree Road in Brookhaven. The house couldn't be seen from the street, but as Milam steered her Jeep down the gravel drive it came into view. The modest two-story structure was well kept and, I was surprised to see, still somebody's home.

"Stop here," I said, reaching for the door handle. "I'll just get a quick picture."

I jumped out where the drive curved in front of the house and started snapping photos as fast as I could, hoping we wouldn't be arrested for trespassing. I climbed back in the Jeep about the same time the front door opened and a woman stepped out.

"I'm sorry. We didn't mean to trespass. We're leaving," I called out the car window. "I just wanted a picture because Solomon Goodwin was my husband's great-great-great-great grandfather."

She gave us a big smile. "He was mine, too. Why don't you come in and I'll show you around?"

Lynda Martin welcomed us into her home, showed us around the place and shared wonderful stories of its history. While Solomon Goodwin's sons had originally traveled from South Carolina to Georgia to find gold, when he followed them a few years later, he was more interested in farming than prospecting. He built this house in 1831 and members of the family have lived there ever since.

The Civil War was especially hard on the Goodwin family. Solomon's two sons were killed in action and, in 1864, some of Sherman's troops headquartered at the house while preparing for the Battle of Atlanta. One of the old mantels still shows the damage where soldiers chipped wood off of it for kindling to start a fire.

For more than 150 years, there was a graveyard adjacent to the house where numerous generations of Goodwins were laid to rest. But in November of 2007, the family moved the graves to the cemetery at nearby Nancy Creek Primitive Baptist Church. It was quite a job, but they knew it was necessary because of encroaching development. Lynda chronicled the entire undertaking and turned it into a book, entitled *Gifts from the Dead: Moving Goodwins Graveyard*. The book was a gift for her father, Albert Lynn Martin, Jr., on his eightieth birthday.

Like the graveyard, the old house itself may soon become a victim of progress. The whole area is now zoned for commercial enterprises and developers don't want a centuries-old structure in the middle of their shopping malls or office buildings. Taxes have risen dramatically since the area has become zoned for commercial development and the Martins have reluctantly put up a For Sale sign. While they know the land will soon be gone, they're hoping someone might take the old house and move it to a location where the community can enjoy this lovely piece of the past.

We said our goodbyes to Lynda and I experienced a sudden sadness. I wished Carl were still alive. He'd have been so proud to

see the house his ancestor built still standing today. I promised myself I'd bring the children and grandchildren to see it as soon as I
could.

Solomon Goodwin House

# The Covered Bridge at Stone Mountain

## JWW

Stone Mountain means different things to different people and the perception of that huge mass of granite rising almost two thousand feet from the earth in eastern DeKalb County has changed over the years. It was a gathering place for native people, the site of Civil War battles and, in the first half of the twentieth century, famous for the enormous high-relief sculpture of Confederate heroes—Jefferson Davis, Robert E. Lee, and Thomas "Stonewall" Jackson—carved into its north face. The carvings took nearly sixty years to complete and are larger than the faces on Mount Rushmore. The locale was also infamous for the Klan rallies and cross burnings held at the base of the mountain.

But that history has been nearly overshadowed by the building of Stone Mountain Park. With its Skyride, Scenic Railroad, lake, and 3-D laser shows, it's become a favorite recreational location for Georgians and tourists alike.

When we visited the park that Friday we weren't planning to scale the mountain, ride the train, or visit the antebellum plantation. We had one goal—we were looking for the covered bridge. We followed Robert E. Lee Boulevard eastward around the base of the mountain. The sun shining on the summit made me remember my visits to the top – several times on the Skyride and twice by the climbing trail. The view from the top had always been worth the trek.

"There it is!" Milam spotted the bridge first.

Viewed through the trees, the old lattice-covered bridge spanning an inlet of Stone Mountain Lake was a romantic sight. It was something from an earlier time where travelers and their horses sheltered from storms, courting couples found a bit of privacy, and highwaymen hid in the rafters to drop down and surprise their victims. The only thing that spoiled this historic illusion was the bright red pickup truck parked at the other end.

While it's now called the Stone Mountain Covered Bridge, this structure began its life in 1891 as a bridge over the Oconee River in Athens, near the University of Georgia campus. It was called both the College Avenue Bridge and the Oconee River Bridge. For dcades it provided the citizens of Athens safe transport from one side of the river to the other. But in the middle years of the last century, it acquired the informal name of Effie's Bridge, after the proprietor of a nearby bordello frequented by college boys. The young men used the bridge as a shortcut to Effie's from the campus.

It was damaged by flood waters and closed down as unsafe in 1963 and was moved to Stone Mountain Park in 1965. The bridge was added to the National Register of Historic Places in 1974.

Covered bridge, Stone Mountain

# Rebecca Latimer Felton

## JWW

In the interest of saving time, we stopped for lunch that day at a fast food restaurant. It didn't meet our usual high standards—there were no vegetables, no cornbread, and definitely no cobbler—but the day was slipping away and we still wanted to drive out to see the birthplace of Rebecca Latimer Felton.

Most people are unaware of the fact that the first female United States Senator was from Georgia. Eighty-one year old Rebecca Latimer Felton was a businesswoman, long-time political activist, suffragist, and temperance advocate when she was appointed to fill a Senate vacancy after the death of Senator Thomas Watson in September of 1922.

Georgia Governor Thomas Hardwick made what he considered the symbolic appointment in October of that year, hoping to soothe the anger he'd caused in the state's new women voters when he'd campaigned against the ratification of the Constitutional amendment giving them the vote. It was an election year, but Felton wasn't on the ballot. Hardwick's plan was for her to stay home and quietly accept the honor, then have the seat filled by the winner of the November election. But Felton and her supporters had other ideas.

Senator Felton surprised everyone when she traveled by train to Washington, DC, in January. Walter George, who had just been elected to the seat, allowed her to enter the Senate chamber ahead of him and be seated, thus becoming the country's first female senator, if only for one day.

Her fellow senators generally ignored her presence, but she wasn't deterred. The next day she made a speech to a large audience, predicting that women would soon take their places not only in the Senate, but in national and local legislative bodies across the country.

"And," she told them, "you will get ability, you will get integrity of purpose, you will get exalted patriotism, and you will get unstinted usefulness."

When we learned about Rebecca Felton, Milam and I knew we had to visit the birthplace of this pioneering woman. We set out from Stone Mountain with what I thought were very clear directions. Once again I was wrong and it didn't help that we missed a couple of exits off I-285 and I-20 and had to backtrack. But we finally found Covington Highway.

It should have been a straight shot from there; but, of course, it wasn't and the U-turns multiplied. Trying to interpret the directions, I was getting a bit testy, but Milam was her usual laid-back self.

"You know," she said as she drove along a back road, "I've been lost out here before, so much of this is familiar to me."

That made me laugh and I suddenly felt better. We were good friends riding around and sharing interesting experiences. How lucky were we?

Although it took longer than expected, we finally found the marker across from a Shell station at the unremarkable intersection of Covington Highway and Wellborn Road. We parked and got out to take pictures as traffic sped by, blowing dust and litter in its wake. I wondered if any of those travelers knew that the country's first female senator had been born right here in 1835, the daughter of pioneer settlers Charles and Eleanor Latimer.

There's much more to learn about Felton and her full, extraordinary life in Louise Staman's fascinating book *Loosening Corsets*.

# Decatur Courthouse, Steatite Boulder, and a Valentine

MMP

Jackie is more the courthouse authority than I, so as we walked toward the historic DeKalb County Courthouse, we decided I'd write about the Steatite Boulder, which is displayed on the building's left side. She'd take on other topics.

As we approached, something else caught my eye. It was a life-size bronze statue featuring an older couple sitting contently on a park bench. Created by the famous sculptor, George Lundeen, the piece is called *Valentine*.

My heart skipped a beat. So touching was the work, I almost cried.

A passerby stopped. "Lovely, aren't they?"

"They are, indeed."

"Very often," she said, "visitors will place a single red rose in their hands."

Putting my hand on my chest, I swooned.

I was a little disappointed to learn later there are several copies of Lundeen's *Valentine* throughout the country, most of which are in private collections. What sets Decatur's sculpture apart, however, is that it's lovingly dedicated to former Decatur mayor Bill Floyd and his wife, Jacquelyn.

Jackie had also become sidetracked. Okay, so I had to say it! She was having her own Lundeen moment. Her favorite U.S. President happens to be Thomas Jefferson. George Lundeen's incredible statue of the third president, seated, signing the Declaration of Independence, was right there beside the sidewalk. So lifelike is he, one can almost hear the scratch of his quill pen.

I snapped a picture of Jackie with Thomas Jefferson. She took mine with the darling couple.

Pleased with our first few moments on the grounds of the old courthouse, we focused on the business at hand, the steatite boulder. According to the historic marker, the large rock before us was at least three thousand years old. It was discovered along Soapstone Ridge, a prehistoric quarry located eight miles south of Decatur. It is believed to be the largest such boulder found by archaeologists in all of Georgia.

As she and I examined the stone, we could easily make out two, maybe three bowls prior to girdling, which is the process of carving objects from stone. Young imaginations take off as today's children visit this site and act out ancient Native Americans creating bowls from these huge boulders.

Before going into the courthouse, I stopped at the statue to pay my respects to the mayor and his wife. Once inside, Jackie and I would have yet another delightful surprise.

Milam and *The Valentine*

Jackie and *Thomas Jefferson*

# Historic DeKalb County Courthouse

## JWW

A courthouse has stood in Decatur, the governmental seat of DeKalb County, since 1823. However, there have been a number of different courthouse buildings, beginning with a crude wooden structure and ending with the historic courthouse that now stands on the square. It was built in 1918 and used until 1967 when the county erected a new courthouse elsewhere.

The old courthouse, which we were visiting that morning, was placed on the National Register of Historic Places in 1971. In 1968, it became the DeKalb History Center and the DeKalb History Museum was opened here in 1983.

We were lucky enough to visit there while they were hosting a special exhibit. *The Mid-Century Ranch House: Hip and Historic!* was waiting for us on the first floor. It replicated a dream home, circa 1960, complete with photos, artwork, and furniture from the period. It was like revisiting our childhoods.

Our trip into the past continued as we returned to the car and drove the short distance to Decatur Cemetery. Burials began taking place here before the city's incorporation in 1825. It now covers fifty-six acres and contains over twenty thousand graves.

We stood near the entrance and admired the peaceful place. Across a small lake lay a hillside where the oldest graves are located. Many distinguished statesmen are buried here, but the cemetery is also host to people of all ethnic origins and social levels. Soldiers from every American war were laid to rest here.

DeKalb County Courthouse

# The Mary Gay House and
# the Swanton House

## MMP

I jumped at the chance to write a short piece about Decatur's Mary Gay House (circa: 1820). Jamey and I attended a delightful wedding reception in the federal style antebellum home and have treasured fond memories of the place ever since.

Born in Milledgeville in 1828, Mary Ann Harris Gay, author, poet, historian, and fundraiser, is best known for penning the book *Life in Dixie During the War*. Highly successful, it went into eleven editions.

In the summer of 1864, Mary Gay adamantly refused to leave the property on which her home originally stood. The Union Calvary under General Kenner Garrard added insult to injury by commandeering Mary's parlor to be used for its headquarters.

On July 22, she and her family, the Stokeses, hid in their cellar and witnessed the skirmishes. It was said the Confederate heroine regretted being prohibited from using firearms during the fighting.

A Yankee officer was quoted as saying to Mary Gay, "I glory in your spunk and am proud of you as my countrywoman."

Her story of the Civil War inspired parts of *Gone with the Wind*.

I like to think of Margaret Mitchell pouring through the pages of *Life in Dixie During the War* making careful notes! It is conceivable Mitchell nodded to herself saying, "Ah ha, this should work beautifully for my book." Maybe, just maybe, she did.

The house in which Mary Gay lived from 1850-1914 was placed on the National Register of Historic Places in 1975. Originally located on Marshall Street, the home was moved to 716 West Trinity Place by the Junior League of DeKalb County in 1979.

Mary Gay passed away at the age of eighty-nine and is buried in Decatur Cemetery. She was named a Georgia Woman of Achievement in 1997.

Jackie and I had a bit of a surprise in store. We'd planned the visit to the Mary Gay House. But, as we were leaving, I wandered next door to see another pretty, white home, the Swanton House.

Originally a log home, built some time prior to 1842, it was first owned by DeKalb County pioneer, Ammi Williams. As I delved into records on the Internet, I discovered that Williams's daughter, Laura Loomis Williams, married Atlanta railroad man, Colonel Lemuel Pratt Grant. He is mentioned in our piece about Ormewood Park. It's always exciting to make these historic connections, not unlike finding all-important corners of a thousand-piece puzzle.

The home was next purchased by Benjamin Franklin Swanton (1807-1890), an early Decatur businessman, who operated a gristmill, tannery, brickyard, and cotton gin. Swanton renovated the home, turning it into the style of an antebellum plantation.

The Swanton House, now owned by the DeKalb History Center, was also relocated from its original land on Peavine Creek to West Trinity Place. Like Mary Gay, members of the Swanton family were in their home when the Federal Army of Tennessee occupied Decatur. The Swanton House also became a Union headquarters.

I was drawn to the back of the property, where I saw two additional buildings, a clapboard structure and a log cabin, which had also been moved to this property. Again online, I discovered the clapboard Biffle Cabin was built as early as 1825, while the log home of Thomas and Martha Barber dates from the 1830s. The official records were destroyed in a huge fire in the DeKalb County Courthouse on January 9, 1842, so there are no exact dates for these historic buildings.

A hitching post also captured my attention because it occupies a place of honor in a brick courtyard surrounded by a small garden.

The hitching post, one of the oldest structures in Decatur, had been in front of the home of Dr. J. H. Goss, Sr. Rumors abound about exactly why the object merits such important status. One thing I like to believe is that some of Decatur's finest people hitched their horses to that post; a "Who's Who" from DeKalb County's richly intriguing past. Oh, but if only we knew for sure.

Ready for lunch, Jackie and I headed to the welcoming square in downtown Decatur. Surely the citizens of those history-rich times were smiling down on us as we enjoyed the lovely place their old town has become.

Mary Gay House

Hitching post at Swanton House

# SHERMAN'S PROGRESS

## CLAYTON COUNTY

The two-day Battle of Jonesboro took place on August 31 and September 1, 1864. The second day ended with Confederate forces withdrawing south and the Federal army, which had flanked the city from the east, moving northward into Atlanta. The city now belonged to Sherman.

# Along the Stagecoach Route in Clayton County

## JWW

We traveled to Clayton County on a Wednesday morning in the first week of August. Although it was the site of the Battle of Jonesboro, which decided the Atlanta Campaign, we were looking for traces of an earlier time—the old stagecoach road, a transportation artery that dated to the early 1800s. We followed the directions to the marker, exiting the expressway at Forest Parkway. Within minutes we were surrounded by subdivisions.

"It's at the corner of Panola Road and Stagecoach Road," I said confidently.

And it was, but it came up quicker than I expected and we had to go down tree-lined Panola Road to a subdivision where I turned around and drove back, pulling to the side of the road near the marker.

"This was it," I told Milam, "the route the stagecoaches used two hundred years ago."

"There's not much to see, is there?"

Gazing up and down Stagecoach Road, the only remnants we saw of the old track that led from Decatur to Columbus were a few ancient trees. The old oaks had, no doubt, seen it change from a pre-Columbian trail to the paved roadway it is today. But with cars whizzing past us, all we could see were neighborhoods of tract houses.

The Rough and Ready Tavern was the next marker on our list and we drove to Mountain View to check it out. The drive should have only taken about ten minutes, but our route ran through a dense industrial area where huge trucks outnumbered cars five to one. At one point, I noticed cars and trucks alike were pulling into the left lane and hurrying around two bright yellow tractor-trailers.

"What's that all about?" Milam asked.

I was just as puzzled as she was until we got close enough to read the big, black letters on one of the trailers: STUDENT DRIVER. Just learning to drive one of the big rigs must have been very difficult, but doing so while trying to maneuver through heavy traffic on narrow streets had to be much, much harder. I wished the student drivers good luck as we slipped past them.

Originally called Rough and Ready, the community of Mountain View got its name because on a clear day you can see Stone Mountain from there. Unfortunately, our day had started out foggy and overcast, and the views were limited.

We drove down a crowded commercial section of Old Dixie Road and, for once, found the marker for the Rough and Ready Tavern with no trouble at all. It was one of four in a row lined up on the side of the road.

The Tavern was long gone, of course, but in the 1840s it had been a stop on the stage line from Macon to north Georgia. In its place was a bright orange building that had been some sort of commercial establishment, but was now empty.

We pulled into the parking lot and got out to see the markers. The setting wasn't ideal. It was almost impossible to reconcile a nineteenth-century inn and tavern with this Day-Glo building as low-flying planes from Hartsfield-Jackson zoomed overhead. I wasn't sure it had been worth the drive and was ready to leave.

But Milam had been reading one of the other markers entitled Transfer Point.

"Did you know about this?" she asked, nearly shouting to be heard over the noise.

I didn't. I went to stand beside her to read the marker. It was a chilling story.

In September of 1864, General Sherman had taken Atlanta, but he was concerned that the citizens might interfere with his troops, so he ordered that the entire civilian population of the city be evicted. Nearly five hundred families, mostly women and children, were forced to leave their homes and their possessions. They could go north or south. Most chose south and were taken in Army wagons to the Rough and Ready Tavern. There, by a truce agreement, they were transferred to Confederate wagons and transported to the railhead of the Macon & Western Railroad where they were released. They were on their own. Neither shelter nor any provision was made for them.

When the mayor of Atlanta complained about such heartless treatment, Sherman simply said, "War is cruelty, and it cannot be refined."

"No wonder people hated the Yankees so much," Milam said.

"Yeah. I guess a lot of this stuff never made it into our eighth-grade Georgia History books."

Site of Rough and Ready Tavern and the Transfer Point

# Sherman's Progress

## Walton, Rockdale, and Newton Counties

While Union forces were closing in on Atlanta in late July 1864, three brigades marched through Walton and Rockdale Counties to Covington in Newton County. There they burned the depot, a new hospital, and large quantities of supplies. They also destroyed two railroad bridges, two wagon bridges, three trains, and six miles of railroad tracks. Atlanta was now completely cut off from Augusta and eastern Georgia.

# The Poppy Lady

## MMP

Jackie and I were enjoying a good many giggles as we added a couple of extra pounds lunching our way through Georgia. We were also picking up some interesting tidbits about our state's history, and, thanks to Jackie's thorough research, were absorbing a fair amount of information about some of its more unique residents, both past and present.

"We're looking for the historic marker for the Poppy Lady," Jackie said.

Poppies? I immediately envisioned Dorothy and Toto, along with the Cowardly Lion, Tin Man, and Scarecrow as they romped through the vast carpet of red poppies in *The Wizard of Oz.*

"Poppy who?"

Jackie pulled off the tree-lined back road in Walton County and parked by a white rail fence. In the distance, a wonderful old barn reminded me of a Fisher-Price farm set. This was a truly gorgeous country with rolling hills, green and lush. The pleasant atmosphere was awash with calm.

"Here, read about Moina Michael. She's responsible for those red poppies distributed every year to recognize war veterans," she said, pointing to the page in our workbook labeled "The Poppy Lady."

As we continued down Highway 83, I read about Moina Belle Michael (1869-1944). Due to her relentless dedication, her campaign established the Flanders Field Poppy as the international symbol for Remembrance of the Veterans of All Foreign Wars. Educated at Braswell Academy and Martin Institute in Jefferson, Georgia, Miss Michael conceived the idea on November 9, 1918, just prior to Armistice Day. At the time, she was serving with the YMCA in New York City.

"There it is."

We jumped from the car and took pictures of one another taking pictures of the historic marker that announced Moina Michael had been born nearby. Jackie noticed that someone had taken the time to tend the small space and had planted a nandina bush between two railroad ties.

A small sign directed us to another spot a mile and a half down Moina Michael Road where a second monument marked the birthplace of Miss Michael. Just before we arrived at her second tribute, we passed a new subdivision called Poppy Field Farm.

"This is more attention than most people will ever receive," said Jackie.

Relishing our find, we snapped a picture and again drove by the sweetly tended historic marker. We turned right and headed for Social Circle.

"It that cotton growing?"

"Too early for cotton, I think," said Jackie. "Looks like white blossoms, hmmm, could be soybeans."

What we were sure about was that Moina's little piece of Georgia was blessed with both beauty and harmony. She'd done all she could to share her gentile upbringing and to honor millions of courageous war veterans. Not bad for a young lady whose first job was teaching school in a log cabin in New Hope.

*Hope*, indeed.

Around Veterans Day next year, when I see the old VFW (Veterans of Foreign Wars) gentleman passing out red plastic poppies at our Kroger, I will tell him about Moina Michael. Likely, he already knows. I'll also be sure to educate Loftin and Emmett about her. I'll buy our grandsons each a poppy to remind them of our veterans including Jackie's father, John Weldon (France, behind enemy lines before D-Day); my father, Bill McGraw (Germany, also WWII); and their grandfather, Jamey (Vietnam).

It is also important to shine a light on the returning veterans of this day, those who are fighting all around the world, particularly in the Middle East. Sometimes we need to put a face on a soldier and his or her family to really appreciate the incredible sacrifices they make for freedom's sake. Nearly every week on the evening news, we learn of someone else we should thank.

This was to be a red-letter eating day for Jackie and me. We were on our way to Social Circle to have a wonderful lunch at the internationally acclaimed Blue Willow Inn Restaurant.

Jackie and I'd both dined at the Blue Willow Inn, and, as expected, that day we were not disappointed with our feast: Southern cuisine at its best. Jackie praised the fried chicken and all three of her dessert choices. Her favorite was the Blue Willow pecan pie, while I went mad for their fried green tomatoes and, of course, the yummy chicken. I topped off my binge by tasting four desserts, the best being lemon meringue pie. We made absolute pigs of ourselves.

A Greek revival mansion, the home originally belonged to Bertha and John Upshaw. In the 1950s, Bertha donated the property to Social Circle to be used as a civic venue. Rich in history, the fine home became a church before Billie and Louis Van Dyke converted it to the inn in 1991.

Seems we talk all too often about *Gone With the Wind*, but, once again, I simply cannot help myself. In a small world moment, I later discovered that Margaret Mitchell was a frequent guest in the Upshaws' home. Her first marriage had been to Redd Upshaw, who was John's cousin. Mitchell based the character of Rhett Butler (played by Clark Gable in the film) on her ex-husband, Redd. I wish I'd known this tidbit when we were at the Margaret Mitchell House!

As we were leaving the Inn, Jackie said, "Don't forget to mention Hightower Trail when you write this story."

Jackie, the adept historian explained Hightower Trail was the old Native American path to the Etowah River, which separated Cherokee and Creek lands.

"Will do."

A little later we saw the historic marker. "November 17-18, 1864, the left wing of Sherman's army passed down the Hightower Trail on the March to the Sea."

I did want to remember the Native Americans, of course, but I did not want to think about Sherman and his ruthless men. I wanted to remember our delightful meal at the Blue Willow Inn. But most importantly, I wanted to think about those who served overseas, especially about the remarkable Georgia native, The Poppy Lady, who continues to honor these brave patriots.

Marker for "The Poppy Lady"

# Zingara

## MMP

I pulled up next to Jackie's car on a September morning. "Good morning. Want me to drive?"

"Nope, hop in."

I pitched my things in the back seat and buckled up. "Where to today?"

"Zingara."

"Say again."

"Zingara."

"Oooookay."

"Zingara, technically it should be pronounced *Zheengara*, is Italian for gypsy woman."

"Zeeengaaara," my Southern accent butchered any attempt at Italian.

We laughed.

"I have another surprise for you," said Jackie, "but you'll have to wait until we get there."

"Goodie, I love surprises."

The first indication this was going to be a stranger than usual journey was when we stopped for a potty break. At first glance, the convenience store in Rockdale County was nothing out of the ordinary. Once inside, however, things changed. The only person in sight was a woman sitting behind a display table guarding an array of NASCAR racing memorabilia.

"Sorry, gals, nothin's for sale," she said. "Y'all can look if you want, but don'tcha dare touch my stuff."

Hands in our pockets, we each took polite glances.

"Very nice."

"Yup. Don'tcha get any closer."

Jackie was just about to ask if she knew if there were a key for the ladies room, when the grinning proprietor, broom in hand, darted out of the facility. He held open the restroom door.

"Bright and shiny clean for you."

Encouraged by his enthusiasm, Jackie went first, while I checked out his assortment of caffeinated colas. I was hoping for a diet Dr. Pepper.

"Proceed at your own risk," warned Jackie. "There are no paper towels, but the smell is, well, unique."

Jackie, who's an herbalist, certainly knows her scents. My curiosity peaked, I stepped inside. GASP!

My tennis shoes instantly stuck to the filthy floor. Had the storekeeper mistakenly mopped with super glue? Struggling to move forward, my shoes made an odd sound, that of releasing a gigantic strip of Velcro.

A gray ring around the nasty sink was so thick it could have supported a bar of soap, had there been one. I had to wonder how many germ-ridden hands had dripped dry throughout the previous months.

What really set the bathroom apart was its interesting odor. Incense? Yes, incense. The wick, some twelve-inches long, emitted a hypnotizing aroma, which not only obscured any disgusting smells, but also served to set the mood for the rest of our day.

Back in the car, we toasted one another with her water and my Dr. Pepper. As we continued through Rockdale County, I looked left.

"Jackie, it that a lighthouse?"

"Sure. Doesn't every major highway need one so the occasional ship can pass safely in the night?" She laughed.

"Or in case of a flood," I added.

This one drew attention to a car wash.

"So what's the surprise?"

"Not until we're there."

Zingara was a pristine community of well-kept houses, white wood fences, and wonderful old barns, horses and chickens, lovely gardens, water wells, steps leading to a long gone home, and a Masonic Lodge.

Outside the lodge, we noticed an elderly couple taking down red, white, and blue holiday decorations. Surely they could tell us the origin of the Zingara name. I stepped from the car, walked toward the lady, and introduced myself. Clearly the petite woman, who was dressed in a soft cotton frock, was apprehensive. Why not? I was quizzing her about gypsies. She likely thought I was of questionable credentials. But Jackie and I persisted, explaining we were writing a book about Georgia and wanted to include their community.

Ann and Weldon Hewatt began to warm to us. Within a couple of minutes, they were bragging happily about the recent big Labor Day barbecue at the Zingara Masonic Lodge.

"Sorry you girls missed it," said Weldon as he ran his fingers through a shock of handsome white hair. "We served eight hundred plates."

As do many long married couples, Ann completed her husband's thoughts. "In years past, we've served as many as twelve hundred."

He, a retired truck driver, added, "We raise money to help out our local families."

"The men cook the meat all the day long," explained Ann. "Weldon spends the entire afternoon pulling pork."

To which he smiled at his wife of some sixty years and said, "In the morning, Ann brings breakfast biscuits for the fellers with fried salmon and ham."

We found out they'd married when Ann was only fifteen and Weldon was eighteen. She giggled and said she landed her first job at Lerner's in Atlanta by telling a little white lie. "I told them I was sixteen years old. Got away with it, too, because I was a married lady."

"My wife's a talker."

Weldon was not only a Mason but also a Shriner. Ever since he retired, with Ann's assistance, he's devoted his life to helping crippled children through the Shriner organization. Unfortunately for the Hewatts, they were not able to have any children of their own. As Ann spoke, I saw the sadness on her face.

"But I'm very blessed," she said. "I was free to care for my youngest sister, Janie. She was born with spina bifida. The doctor said she'd only live for six weeks to six months, but our Janie fooled them. She passed away at age sixty-five. Janie was even able to have a child, a son."

Jackie and I may never learn why Zingara was so named. We may not have found the first gypsy descendant, but we met the Hewatts, truly fine people, a couple with much love to share.

Oh, and one other thing about Ann. She'd had a manicure and pedicure for the Labor Day festivities. Ann's fingernails and toenails were painted a patriotic red. On each of her big toe's nails the pedicurist wrote her name, facing forward so guests could look down and know they were speaking to one genuinely caring lady named Ann.

Waving, we drove away.

"Ready for the surprise now?" asked Jackie.

"Sure."

Jackie explained that thinking about the gypsy woman had encouraged her long-time interest in fortune telling, specifically Tarot cards, so she did an amateur reading for the two of us, focusing on this travel book. She wrote down the results and gave me the complete list. I must admit, it was amazingly accurate. In the interest of space, I'll list just a few of her spot-on findings.

*We are strong but are sometimes overburdened with too many commitments. We are doing the unexpected and have thought much about travel. Creativity is in the air with new people, new places, and a journey. Sometimes we lack focus. We both have problems with authority and occasionally overindulge.*

Jackie made note of "overindulge" and quickly pointed out we might need to cut back on our lunches.

*Best of all, our hard work will be rewarded – eventually!*

Perhaps the gypsy was found. She isn't from Zingara after all.

Jackie White lives in Hoschton, Georgia.

Zingara Masonic Lodge

# Conyers

## MMP

The mere mention of the word "Conyers" produces a rush of pleasant memories for me. The Monastery of the Holy Spirit, not terribly far from downtown Conyers, occupies a niche in my own history.

Growing up in Atlanta, my parents and I often enjoyed the marvelous breads baked by the Trappist monks of Holy Spirit. As a child I'd envision the hallowed gentlemen bringing their bakery items to our church in ancient mule-drawn wagons.

When I was in high school, Daddy and I once traveled out to the monastery in search of a unique Christmas present for my mother. We finally settled on a lovely painting of The Madonna. Momma was elated. The painting hung over her bed until she passed away.

As adults, Jamey and I took our three children to the 2,300-acre property for a Sunday picnic. A few years later, during a quiet moment beside the monastery's tranquil pond, a seed was planted in me to alter our lives and send our children to Catholic schools.

On another occasion, I rode to Conyers with my friend, Ave Bransford, and there we spent a memorable day together. And, it's certainly no coincidence that my favorite priest, Father Steve Yander, finds the monastery to be a perfect place for reflection. Father says the peace-filled atmosphere nourishes his soul.

While driving through Rockdale County with Jackie, I sensed the monastery calling to me. I felt compelled to introduce her to the Monastery of the Holy Spirit.

"You'll appreciate the serenity of this place." I added, "I can't wait for you to see the beautiful swans."

It wasn't difficult to convince her to go.

As a result, we didn't do justice to the fine town of Conyers. We did, however, drive slowly through Old Towne and admire its charming antique shops and restaurants, a converted railroad station now turned visitors center, and delightful green spaces, one of which showcases an authentic Dinky (steam locomotive) Engine.

Because our side trip came as a surprise to Jackie, an ever-organized travel planner, we had to stop for directions. Not that it made a difference given my dreadful sense of direction, but I'd always been a passenger and never took note of how I got anywhere.

I went into a convenience store while Jackie waited in the car. As things tend to happen to us, the fellow there spoke not one word of English. Even so, he finally realized we were looking for the monastery. My pious pose as I made the sign of the cross gave him a clue. He pointed toward I-20 and indicated the monks were but a couple of minutes away. Looking back, he may have said, "Mucho miles."

On we drove, on and on and ON. I nervously picked at my fingernails.

"Are you sure he said to turn left?"

"Absolutely," I lied.

Then the miracle occurred. "Look, Jackie, the sign says 'Monastery.' It's pointing straight ahead!"

I took a deep, cleansing breath, and vowed to work on my Spanish.

Sure enough, the thoughtful monks of Holy Spirit must have realized pilgrims such as Jackie and myself would need guidance, because each time we worried we'd somehow passed our destination, another sign would appear.

"We're here!"

I was amused by the sight of two monks, who, garbed in long black and white robes, were bouncing along a path in a golf cart.

Immediately wishing we'd set aside an entire day to drink in the slowed pace of the welcoming monastery, we settled down to a delicious lunch in the abbey's Garden Cafe. We toured the grounds, stopping in for a visit to the magnificent Gothic church. I was astounded to read that the monks had constructed the entire building, including the church's stunning stained glass windows.

I picked up a brochure as we left the church to find out what is available for visitors. The highlights include talks and tours by the monks themselves, weekend retreats with space for forty-five people, a world class Bonsai garden, and thirty miles of nature trails. Hikers often come across a deer or a wild turkey as they walk the lush pathways. There's also the Monastic Heritage Center, which shares the remarkable story of the Cistercian monks (Trappist order), who, in 1944, founded the Rockdale County monastery.

I suggested we check out the gift shop. As expected, there were numerous religious items and books along with delights such as honey from the abbey's hives, homemade fudge, and the monks' famous fruitcake and breads, but something else caught our eyes.

Handing the clerk our credit cards, we each purchased peasant-style blouses.

"I've never owned anything made in Kathmandu," said Jackie.

"Well worth our change of plans?"

"I think so!"

We never spotted a single swan, but that was okay. Perhaps the regal swans were a figment of my imagination just like the mule-drawn wagons.

Interior of the church at the Monastery of the Holy Spirit

# Baseball, Colleges, Vampires, and Ice Cream

## JWW

After Conyers, we traveled to Newton County. Milam was impressed with the rural scenery.

"It's just beautiful," she said more than once.

She was right. We passed pastures and dairy farms and little settlements that might or might not have been towns.

Mansfield falls into the town category. As of the 2010 census, 371 people made it their home. The locals call the place "Newton County's Front Porch" and it boasts a number of pretty houses—complete with fine front porches—a couple of business blocks, and a small manufacturing company.

Milam pointed out a barbecue place called Soda Pop's. She liked the name and I suspected she wouldn't have said no to sampling it, even though lunch was only an hour before. Tiny as she is, Milam's always hungry. I, on the other hand, probably gained a pound or two just breathing the air around the restaurant. I don't think it's fair.

"They also have a historical marker," I said to distract her.

The marker that sits on the side of Highway 11 is titled Mansfield's Famous Southpaw and honors Sherrod Malone Smith, who played fourteen seasons in the big leagues during baseball's golden age. Smith was an acclaimed pitcher. Babe Ruth once said "He's the greatest pick-off artist who ever lived." Smith was inducted into the Georgia Sports Hall of Fame in 1980 and he and his wife are both buried in Mansfield.

Continuing our tour of Newton County, we found the town of Oxford and a marker commemorating the founding of Emory College by the Georgia Methodists in 1837. In 1919, Emory moved to its current Atlanta location and this campus where we stood became

Oxford College. It's now one of Emory University's nine academic divisions.

We wandered around for a while. Students still enthused with the beginning of the term hurried between buildings. With its immaculate brick structures and green lawns, it seemed like the kind of place you'd like to send your children. But for casual day-trippers like us, there wasn't anything remarkable to see. It seemed unlikely we were going to find one of those quirky little stories we enjoyed so much here and I thought this might have been a wasted trip. Milam agreed.

"Maybe it's time to call it a day," I said, "but I want ice cream before we go home."

"I could go for that."

We were close to Covington, so we crossed Interstate 20 and headed for the little town that had become famous as the location for the television series *In the Heat of the Night*. Since then countless movies and TV shows had been filmed here.

We passed the usual business districts and neighborhoods.

"Oh, look at those trucks."

I glanced where Milam was pointing and saw a couple of white utility trucks parked behind a business. The word *Lightning* was written across them along with some other words I couldn't read.

"What about them?"

"They're just like the ones they used on our movie."

For those readers who aren't aware of it, one of Milam's books was made into the movie *The Adventures of Ociee Nash*. She and her husband Jamey spent a lot of time on the set and each made a brief appearance in the film. Ever since then she's been very conscious of anything involving filmmaking.

Covington has a picturesque town square, but as I turned right to start the circuit around it, my focus was firmly on ice cream and there on the opposite corner of the street, just as if it were planned, was an ice cream shop! I whipped the car into a parking place facing the square.

"Ice cream!"

As you can see, I have my priorities in order, but Milam was distracted as we got out of the car.

"What's going on over there?" she asked, pointing to the far side of the square where a number of people milled around.

In the distance we heard someone shout, "Quiet!" Then a moment later, "Action!"

Milam lit up like a sunrise. "They're shooting a movie!"

That's when I noticed huge cables running all over the place. About then a big yellow school bus passed us. But instead of Newton County Schools it had Mystic Falls painted on the side.

"Ice cream," I said determinedly and started across the street.

Milam wasn't as enthusiastic as I was, but followed, walking backward much of the time so she could keep an eye on the activity across the square.

We each ordered a scoop of ice cream (peach for me). As the young man behind the counter took my money, I asked, "What are they filming here this time?"

"*Vampire Diaries.*" He sounded bored. I guess the natives have seen so many film projects that they don't get excited about them anymore.

This wasn't true of Milam. She was completely star-struck. We sat in rocking chairs outside the shop and she rarely took her eyes off the film crew.

When she took her last bite of ice cream, she said, "Let's walk around the square. Maybe we'll overhear them talking."

Which is just what we did. At one point, we passed two men in earnest conversation. Milam slowed for a moment, straining to hear what was being said.

A few steps later, she whispered, "They're talking about shooting on location at an old mill!" She had an excited gleam in her eyes and I knew what she was thinking.

"Oh, no, we're not going to do that. We can't follow these people around." She was crestfallen, but I was firm. "They're liable to call the police and have us arrested for stalking."

She sighed. "Oh, okay."

We returned to the car—me happy at having ice cream and Milam excited about another brush with Hollywood. We both agreed that it hadn't been a wasted trip.

*Vampire Diaries* school bus

Film crews at work, Covington

# Burge Plantation

## MMP

There's a little piece of Heaven along our route to Savannah, a place Jackie and I have come close to several times on our research jaunts.

Every time, I announce, "That's the turnoff to Burge Plantation." I mention our friends, Pam and David Weeks, and speak of their generosity in sharing their hunting club with lucky people including me.

I've had the pleasure of going to Burge with Pam and our lady friends. We girls have driven and walked about the plantation's grounds with its wooded acres, hunting fields, and lush organic vegetable gardens. We've toured the well-curated family museum, played bridge on a sun-warmed porch, dined in the classic manor, "the big house," checked out the guest cottages, and giggled into the wee early hours of the morning.

On one occasion, we took a cooking course from Burge's amazing Chef Andrew. To begin our class, he invited us to meander through his organic herb garden. Andrew offered me a pinch of lavender. I can still remember its delicious scent.

I've participated in just about everything but what most members of this private hunting club come to do. I haven't shot a gun since I earned my riflery badge at Camp Marymount in 1955.

In 1809, Wiley Burge obtained the original two hundred plus acres through a land grant. Now some nine hundred and thirty acres in size, Burge Plantation belongs to Betsy and Sandy Morehouse. He is the sixth generation of family to tend the property; she is the resident historian. Their three daughters, and their families bring the number of generations to eight.

After spending time with Betsy and Sandy, it is abundantly clear that their stories, hundreds of interesting stories, could fill volumes. Alas, I must confine this piece to a few short pages. However, much has already been published about Burge, including *A Woman's Wartime Journal* by Dolly Sumner Lunt Burge. It's on her work I feel compelled to focus.

A native of Maine, Dolly was a widowed schoolteacher, who married Thomas Burge in 1850. She kept a detailed diary from1848 to 1879. A fascinating portion spans just days short of a year, January 1, 1864 to December 25, 1864. Dolly chronicles Sherman's March to the Sea. General Sherman himself was leading the 14th Corps of the Left Wing straight through the heart of Burge Plantation.

Dolly's words: "...like Demons they run in. My yards are full. To my smoke house, my Dairy, Pantry, kitchen, and cellar like famished wolves they come, breaking locks and whatever is in their way."

In November of 1864, Dolly stood with her nine-year-old daughter Sadai as Sherman's troops trampled her farm, even killing her livestock. Dolly writes of their taking her favorite carriage horse, Old Dutch, which had borne to his grave the body of her late husband, Thomas Burge. There's something soul wrenching in reading in Dolly's own words about how the general's men tore down her fences and desolated her home, "when there was no necessity for it."

Local lore tells a tale of Sherman's horse drinking from the well, which remains to this day. It's just to the left of the main house.

Recently, when Jackie and I met with our publisher Marc Jolley, he suggested we write how our journey might have changed something about us. For me, it was the trip to Burge. Dolly's journal placed real people into those tragic days. No longer were the historic markers simply dates about soldiers and their battles. After reading *A Woman's Wartime Journal*, I envisioned the young children and women like myself standing up to a terrifying enemy. This was a chilling revelation.

I walked the hallowed grounds of Burge. I paused in the family cemetery. I spent a night in the big house studying family pictures and the art and keepsakes of centuries past. Suddenly the dry pages of history books transformed as the Burge ancestors came to life. Dolly's personal account of thousands of Sherman's men destroying her farm transported me back to horrific scenes of THE WAR.

Dr. Jolley was right. My outlook was altered.

Then there was the wedding cup. As we sat sipping coffee by the morning fire, our friend Betty noticed a sweet old photograph of a turn-of-the-century bride. Placed beside her picture was a small silver chalice.

Cup in my hand, I read that the lovely young lady, Ida Eve Gray, was the bride of Merritt Morehouse. Familiar names, the two would eventually become Sandy's grandparents. The silver heirloom had played a part in family weddings since the 1700s.

But for a time, it went missing. As the story goes, a loyal slave buried the chalice along with the family silver and other valuables to keep them safe from Yankee looters. When the war was finally over, life slowly returned to the new normal of mourning and efforts to heal.

At long last, there would again be weddings at Burge Plantation. The precious cup was assumed to be yet another casualty of war.

As one ceremony was about to get underway, a caring servant named Eneas jumped from his mule-drawn wagon. He was clutching a small object in his hand. The chalice! His determination to find the piece came in the nick of time. Thanks to Eneas, the family tradition was restored.

Family tradition, indeed. That's what Burge is all about, especially in its latest incarnation. The present day plantation, a private hunting preserve since 1981, has become a place ripe for building memories with families and friends.

One story I want to share is about Sandy Morehouse himself. As we sat chatting in the parlor of the home built by his grandfather Merritt Morehouse, an architect, Sandy talked about a gentle black man whom he knew as Teemie. Working hard throughout the week, Teemie always preached on Sundays at Parks Grove School and Church.

Betsy quickly added, "Sandy's grandmother, Ida Eve Gray Morehouse, had the Parks Grove building constructed in 1910."

I noted the date.

"Thanks, Betsy," said Sandy. A pleasant smile crossed his face. "Teemie pretty much took me under his wing,"

As a young lad, the current steward of Burge loved to visit his grandparents. Of course, one of the first things Sandy did was look for Teemie. He and the old black fellow would take a wagon filled with trash to be discarded. This was the *new* method we now call "recycling." Sandy says he delighted in depositing garbage in compost piles.

"I can still see myself, oh, age five or so, sitting proudly next to Teemie as his mule Pete pulled our wagon."

I asked if the wagon were still there. Sandy answered with, "Yes, or one just like it."

Sandy's eyes sparkled with his happy memory.

"As a grown man, I could walk into our barn. Obviously, Teemie is long gone," he recalled, "but I can still recognize the pleasant and familiar scent of my old companion."

Betsy Morehouse is a jewel in the Morehouse crown. Not only does she cherish Burge, she has also organized a wonderful museum in the two-room house where Teemie raised his own family.

There's more.

Betsy has created a second museum in the top level of the big house. Her "Burge Attic Game," is a scavenger hunt, which encompasses two hundred plus years of antique toys, furniture, art, items of clothing, travel and sports memorabilia, record albums, and one creepy, old wheelchair. Betsy's list of objects to discover provides adventure for both children and adults.

Burge is a time capsule, a place for sport and delicious cuisine, a place for study, a place for relaxing in nature, and a place for family.

I went to Burge for a birthday celebration for friends whom Jackie White doesn't know. It was my only research trip without her I thought often of my co-author. She'd have loved Burge.

My concern is when we do go there together, perhaps for a book signing, Jackie White will simply refuse to leave this remarkable place! It is right up her alley. It's right up my alley, too.

Main house at Burge Plantation

Well at Burge Plantation

# Sherman's Progress

## Morgan, Greene, And Putnam Counties

After destroying Atlanta, Sherman divided his Army into two wings. The right wing went south, appearing to have Macon as a destination. On November 18, 1864, the left wing of Sherman's Army marched from Social Circle to Madison, destroying the railroad as they went. In Rutledge, they burned the depot, the water tank, and several warehouses. And the next day, they destroyed the railroad bridge over the Oconee River.

Although the same Federal troops occupied Greensboro in Greene County for several hours on Sunday, November 20, they marched on without disturbing the six hospitals for Confederate soldiers that had been set up in various buildings in the town. On the 21st they passed through Eatonton in Putnam County. They did tear up several miles of railroad track there, but the bad weather—torrential rains that turned the roads to nearly impassable mud—prevented them from visiting further destruction on Putnam County.

# Madison

## JWW

Put simply, Madison is a lovely town with antebellum and Victorian homes, intriguing little shops, and restaurants that should definitely be sampled. Milam and I rolled into town that morning and circled the square a couple of times. Driving in circles wasn't anything new for us, but this time we had an excuse. We were taking it all in. Even in early September, when the northern half of the country is feeling autumn's first chill, middle Georgia is warm and, often, hot. That Wednesday, summer's multi-colored zinnias still bloomed on the corners of the square and the streets were filled with people who hadn't yet put away their warm-weather clothes.

"You know, Sherman refused to burn this town," I told Milam.

"Why?"

I was stuck. I'd heard stories, but didn't really know why. So we stopped at the Welcome Center to get the facts.

While the legend is that the fire-happy general refused to burn the town because it was so beautiful, the truth is that resident Joshua Hill met with Sherman on the outskirts of Madison and reminded him that he was friends with the general's brother. The two came to a "gentleman's agreement" to spare the town.

The kind woman at the Welcome Center suggested that we might enjoy a driving tour of the town.

"You'll see a lot more that way than trying to walk everywhere," she said and handed us a simple map of the historic district. The route was clearly marked.

With our record on navigation, we should have known better; but, if nothing else, we're always optimistic. We backed out of the parking space and took a quick right on North Main Street. Milam drove while I tracked our progress on the map.

"We should cross Second Street right up here," I predicted.

But we didn't. Frantically looking for landmarks and checking and rechecking the map, we were completely lost in minutes. After a few turnarounds, we worked our way back to the Welcome Center and pulled into the same parking place we'd had before.

Together we pored over the map. It only took us about five minutes – and a belated look at the street signs – to realize I'd been holding it upside down the whole time. So ... we began again.

Driving the correct route this time, we found some interesting spots – museums, churches and, of course, historical homes. We even came across a marker on the square dedicated to Oliver Hardy, the legendary comedian who lived in Madison as a child when his mother operated a hotel here. You never know what you're going to find!

Welcome center, downtown Madison

# Greensboro

## JWW

We drove from Madison to Greensboro where there were two markers we wanted to see. They were both law-enforcement related.

Greensboro is a pleasant, well-kept town, which made our initial sighting of the Old County Gaol that much more unsettling. Even the quaint spelling of jail couldn't soften the impression it made. My first thought was that it was a hard, cold, frightening building. Constructed in 1807 of local granite, it must have caused to drop a prisoner's heart as he was led through that massive wooden door.

As Milam read aloud from the marker, my first impressions were reinforced. The cells were described as dungeons without light or ventilation. On the second floor was a trap door to facilitate the hangings that were carried out there. The jail was in use until 1895.

We strolled around the corner to the L. L. Wyatt Museum. The marker in front of the old building had been erected in honor of Loy Lee Wyatt who enforced the laws of Georgia and Greene County for fifty-two years. According to the marker, Wyatt joined the Greene County Police Department in 1925 and began a fifteen-year, one-man war against moonshiners. When he'd cleaned up the illicit liquor business, he was elected sheriff.

Although wounded five times, he never lost a gunfight, including one in 1970 when he shot it out with a carload of bank robbers. When Wyatt died in office in 1977, he'd served more than half a century as a peace officer.

I kept trying to imagine what he might have looked like, but my mind was cluttered with pictures of all the actors who'd played famous real life lawmen – Kurt Russell as Wyatt Earp, Joe Don

Baker as Buford Pusser, Johnny Cash as Lamar Potts. I don't know who'd be right to play L. L. Wyatt, but the story ought to be told.

Old Greene County Gaol

# Fort Mathews and Elijah Clarke

## JWW

I'm an admitted history geek and have always been fascinated by this story, so the day we were in Greenesboro, I insisted we drive out of town to find the Fort Mathews marker where Highway 278 crosses the Oconee River. For once we had no trouble finding the spot and pulled onto the shoulder so we could get out for a better look.

Peeking through the trees and scrub out to the Oconee River and the wooded shore beyond, it was almost like seeing the wilderness Georgia was a part of in 1794. Back then only a few forts had been constructed on the edge of the frontier. One of these was Fort Mathews.

White settlers were forbidden to cross the Oconee River. Doing so would violate a treaty with the native tribes in the area. But Elijah Clarke, a Revolutionary War hero, did just that when he and the band of settlers he led established several forts between the Flint and Oconee Rivers in Creek Territory. They were intent on forming their own nation called the Trans-Oconee Republic and had even written their own constitution. From these forts, Clarke and his land-hungry followers attacked nearby Creek villages.

Thomas Houghton, a justice of the peace at Fort Mathews, sent word to Georgia Governor George Mathews, advising him of what was going on. Mathews, in turn, notified Washington. Secretary of War Henry Knox ordered him to stop Clarke.

Mathews ordered Clarke to dismantle the settlements and bring his people back across the Oconee. When Clarke refused, the Georgia militia was sent to enforce the order. That show of force convinced Clarke and his settlers to surrender without a shot being fired, and the Trans-Oconee Republic was no more.

Site of Fort Mathews

# Brer Rabbit, Jackie, and Me

## MMP

There are perfect days and there are super perfect days. This Wednesday in early October ranked in the super perfect category.

On Monday, I had taken Loftin to the Atlanta History Center. Jamey and I have been members for years; I often question why everyone in the vicinity doesn't join. Loftin and I walked up to the Swan House, and, at his insistence, wandered back through the Tullie Smith Farm.

"Remember when you brought Emmett and me here for the sheep shearing?"

"Sure do."

"We watched every step from shearing and cleaning the sheep's wool to making a shawl. After, we got ice cream."

We grandmothers love for our grandchildren to spend time with us, especially when they can experience something educational and unique. Most grandmothers like ice cream, too.

Loftin and I decided to spend the majority of our day in the history museum. I wanted him to see the displays about his city's past, its pioneers and people, industries and businesses, and its resilience and revered position as the "City Too Busy to Hate."

I reminded him of the book Jackie and I were writing about Sherman's March to the Sea. As a Southerner, I find it uncomfortable to discuss the Civil War with my grandson, especially regarding the issue of slavery, but I tried to be honest and answered his questions as best I could.

On a lighter note, he and I enjoyed the display about Joel Chandler Harris, author of the Uncle Remus stories, 1848-1908. I told Loftin that Jackie and I were going to visit the famous author's birthplace and I promised to pick up some Uncle Remus books for him and Emmett.

On Wednesday, Jackie and I arrived in Eatonton and pulled up in front of the Uncle Remus Museum. It's located just across the street from Putnam County Elementary School. How fortunate are those girls and boys to have such a marvelous place to visit so nearby.

In front of the log cabin structure is a delightful sculpture of Brer Rabbit, which reads, "Born and Bred in the Briarpatch, he survives forever by his wit, his courage, and his cunning."

We were greeted by docent Donna Crouch, who spoke with us about the legacy of Eatonton's famous author, of the museum, and of nearby Turnwold Plantation.

"Our building is made up of three original slave quarters from Putnam County, which have been joined together. We've tried to gather as many artifacts as we can to give visitors a better understanding of what life was like during the plantation era."

Using actual slave quarters as the museum site is particularly appropriate because the Uncle Remus stories came from fables passed down through African slaves. Jackie and I absorbed the flavor of those long gone times as we strolled among the rag dolls and toys, kitchen items, cookie cutters, dishes, and tools. We also looked at samples of Harris's books. According to Mrs. Crouch, his books have been printed in some thirty or forty languages. Significantly, Joel Chandler Harris's stories are recognized as the largest single collection of African American folktales ever published.

At the tender age of thirteen, Joel Chandler Harris became an apprentice at Turnwold Plantation, which was owned by Joseph Addison Turner. Young Joel flourished under the guidance of this gentleman, who would become his teacher, his mentor, and a father figure. Not only did Harris learn the trade of typesetting while working on Turner's newspaper, *The Countryman*, but the eager student also made his initial steps into a lifelong career, first as a newspaper reporter, and later on, as an author.

Throughout his years at Turnwold, Joel spent many a night sitting in front of roaring fires listening to the extraordinary narratives told by the slaves of Turnwold Plantation. One slave was Uncle George Terrell, whose portrait hangs in the museum. Uncle George is one of the gifted storytellers on which Joel Chandler Harris's Uncle Remus character is based.

Harris moved to Savannah, where he worked for the *Savannah Morning News* from 1870-1876. He married the daughter of a French sea captain. They had nine children, six of whom survived to adulthood.

In 1878, once Harris firmly established himself as a journalist at *The Atlanta Constitution*, he decided to include one of the animal fables in his newspaper column. He wrote the story using authentic Geechee dialect. Readers couldn't get enough of these tales that taught while making them laugh or scratch their heads. Soon people from around the world were reading stories about human nature in the guise of rabbits, foxes, bears, and their friends and foes.

The Wren's Nest is the Atlanta home of the world famous author. Located in Historic West End next to St. Anthony's Catholic Church, the Harris home remains exactly as it was when he passed away in 1908.Yet another must-see spot in Atlanta, visitors can schedule time to hear a storyteller share a tale of Brer Rabbit, Brer Fox, or Brer Bear, most often told in the Geechee dialect.

"The Tar Baby" has always been my favorite.

Uncle Remus Museum, Eatonton

# Rock Eagle Mound

## JWW

The Rock Eagle 4-H Center north of Eatonton on Highway 441 was our last stop of the day. It had turned cooler, making us realize that autumn was in fact underway. Falling leaves drifted around our car as we left the highway and followed a series of twisting roads, directed by wooden signs, to the clearing where the Rock Eagle Effigy Mound lay behind a tall, chain-link fence. On the far side of the mound, looking like a medieval relic plunked down right there in middle Georgia, was a stone observation tower.

We couldn't see much of the effigy from ground level because it was on an elevated plateau, so we walked around the fence to the tower.

"We should be able to see the eagle from the top," I said, leading the way up the massive wooden steps.

Milam was right behind me. "I should tell you I have a terrible fear of heights."

I looked back, wondering if she would faint or retreat, but she stuck with me—all the way up six flights of steps to the top floor of the tower. The wind whistled through the barred openings on the sides of the structure. Milam overcame her fear and joined me at the windows. Clouds had covered the afternoon sun and it was cold in the tower. The height gave us a fairly good view of the eagle, but even from that vantage point, it was hard to see all of it.

Fashioned from hundreds of milky quartz rocks by native people centuries before Columbus ventured across the Atlantic, the effigy is huge, measuring 120 feet from wingtip to wingtip. Looking down, we tried to imagine how long it took for the ancient builders to construct the image. Why they built it was a mystery.

"Maybe it was a burial mound," I wondered aloud, "or had some religious use."

"It might have been built to signal aliens," Milam suggested.

Whatever the reason, it was an impressive sight. But the cold was penetrating and we were both close to shivering. It was time to go.

Rock Eagle mound

Observation tower above Rock Eagle mound

# Sherman's Progress

## Henry, Jasper, and Butts Counties

On November 17, 1864, the right wing of Sherman's Army marched through McDonough in Henry County to the town of Jackson in Butts County. Two divisions went into Jackson and, using pontoon bridges, began ferrying soldiers and equipment across the Ocmulgee River into Jasper County. Another division passed around Jackson and entered Indian Springs where they waited until they, too, could cross the Ocmulgee River. Bad weather hampered the crossing and it wasn't completed until November 20. The army briefly camped in and around Monticello, then continued south toward Milledgeville.

# McDonough

## MMP

"Look out!" I shrieked. I threw my arms over my head and prayed.

"Don't be so dramatic," said Jackie. "That truck wasn't even close."

"You didn't see it from the passenger's side." I had a flashback of riding with my inexperienced teenaged drivers.

"You're overreacting, Milam. We saved time by making a simple U-turn. I can't believe how poorly the entrance ramp to the expressway is marked."

I said no more. On our travels, Jackie does most of the driving. A retired police officer, I must admit she's better than I. Faster, too. And skilled; her adept U-turn was an example.

We were on our way to Shingleroof Campground. Located three miles from McDonough in Henry County, the one hundred-acre site was purchased in 1831 by the Trustees of the Methodist Campmeeting Ground for $280.

The old campground in Sandy Springs (Fulton County) that I wrote about earlier has been gone for more than a century, so I never dreamed we'd find a place that still holds camp meetings. As we turned into Shingleroof, I was taken aback by the beauty of its surrounding woods. Ancient oak trees beckoned for us to come inside. Two jet-black crows frolicked above our car.

A circle of buildings, appearing like the brethren, surrounds a wooden open-air church and dining area. Twenty plus named or numbered cottages, some rustic with sawdust entries, others modern with decks and porches, are painted in vibrant colors. All convey feelings of hope and joy. Swings, rocking chairs, barbeque smokers, and nearby campsites make the grounds feel family friendly. The old shingle roofs have been replaced with tin. How soothing the sound of gentle rain dancing on those cabins on a lazy summer afternoon must be.

The caretaker's dog barked, but his was a welcoming sound. We didn't see any people other than one couple taking a leisurely stroll. I could envision the many folks who come in summertime for peaceful retreats, family reunions, and a time to reflect in a Christian environment.

Jackie, who loves music, commented, "Can you imagine the fine kind of singing you'd hear out here!"

We discovered three gazebos positioned by the side of a small, quiet stream. A granite bench called to me. I paused for a moment to read its chiseled words, "Whoever drinks the water I give him will never thirst." For me, the whole place was awash with serenity. But all too soon, it was time to leave.

Shingleroof has a website with dates, pictures, and information about the facility and the annual encampment.

"Hungry?"

"Always."

We drove to McDonough and found a parking place on the town square. The afternoon was pleasant for November. Jackie snapped a picture of the Henry County Courthouse. Erected in 1823, the stately building was completed in 1897. The statue of a Civil War hero stands sentry. Henry County was named for the patriot Patrick Henry, best known for his immortal words, "Give me liberty, or give me death."

I noticed a spot called Gritz. The family restaurant was peopled with local patrons, specifically with officers of the law. Policemen traditionally know the best places to eat.

Jackie ordered delicious potato soup, while I went with a homemade tuna salad sandwich. We both splurged, gobbling up every bite of hot pecan pie. Not only was Gritz yummy enough to write about, but we also appreciated our darling waitress. She called Jackie "honey bun."

"Ordinarily, that would have irritated me," said my writing buddy. "But since she's calling everybody in here either honey bun or honey, I don't feel like she's singling me out because of my age."

I told Jackie a story of when we first moved from Birmingham to Atlanta. Lonesome for small town Southernisms, we drove up to a Shoney's in Cumming for lunch. The waitress jotted down our orders and said, "I'll be right back with your sweet tea, honey."

This day felt every bit as good.

Shingleroof Campground

# Almanac

## JWW

Before visiting the site of Robert Grier's home in Butts County, it seemed only right that we have a copy of Grier's Almanac – which he began in 1807 and is still in publication today. The Barnes & Noble near my house had almanacs, but not Grier's and it wasn't available through Amazon either. However, the Grier's website suggested copies could be found at pharmacies, feed and seed stores, and general stores. As we drove south from McDonough to Butts County, I asked Milam to help me keep an eye out for those kinds of businesses.

"Killer swine!" she suddenly shouted, scaring me so much I nearly ran off the road.

"*What?*" I asked, regaining control.

"There," she pointed to a distant billboard. "Killer Swine."

I know we were both picturing creatures from some cable TV series until we got close enough to see the smaller print.

"Oh, it's a barbecue restaurant," Milam said, laughing. "I guess I was just startled because I was chased by one once."

That revelation led to a great story. It had happened in Louisiana when she was four or five years old. She and her parents were attending a company picnic out in a rural area and Milam had wandered off by herself into the woods. A few minutes later, she ran screaming back to the gathering.

"A wild boar chased me out of the woods!"

"I can honestly say you're the only person I've ever met who had a close encounter with a wild boar."

Continuing our search for an almanac seemed kind of anti-climactic after that, but we kept looking. It wasn't until we got to the small town of Locust Grove (named for locust trees, not vora-cious grasshoppers) that Milam spotted what we needed.

"There. A pharmacy."

We'd nearly passed it, but I whipped into the parking lot at the last minute. (I just ignored those horns behind us.)

The folks in Moye's Pharmacy couldn't have been nicer. They told us they carried it and, when they found the display rack was empty, looked around the store and came up with a couple of copies of Grier's Almanac. It was last year's edition, but we didn't mind. We took both copies. Now we just had to find the marker.

We uncharacteristically found it on our first try – on the right-of-way in front of a BP store on Stark Road. Unfortunately, the marker was the only trace of Grier's nineteenth century home. But we did have our copies of his almanac. So we spent a little time checking them out and discovered a lot of stuff. The gestation peri-od for mares is 340 days and root crops should be planted while the moon is waning. There was an article about designing water-wise landscapes and ads in the back for seeds, wine and beer making, and psychics.

There was more to see in Butts County, but it was growing late and we wanted to be north of Atlanta before the afternoon traf-fic jams started. Unfortunately, we didn't leave for home early enough. Traffic was bad that afternoon. It would be several weeks before we came back this way.

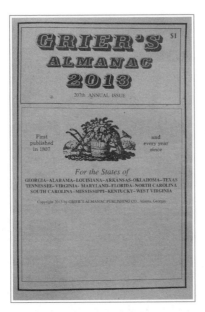

*Grier's Almanac* cover

Milam, Jackie, and "Little Debbie" in Atlanta traffic

# Indian Springs

## JWW

Our first stop on that unusually warm January day was Indian Springs State Park in Butts County. It's lovely, peaceful, and one of the oldest state parks in the country. The springs have been famous for centuries for their healing waters. Visitors today can sample those waters in the Spring House. The park also offers swimming, boating, picnicking, and camping, although we didn't experience any of those pursuits the day we were there. Even though it was warm, it was still January.

We did, however, park the car and stroll through the little village beside the park. We passed shops, restaurants, galleries, and the Whimsical Botanical Garden. It was here in Indian Springs that William McIntosh, chief of the Lower Creeks, built his house in the early 1800s. The house no longer stands, but the inn he constructed is still extant. This graceful building with sweeping double verandahs now houses the Indian Springs Hotel Museum.

Chief McIntosh was one of the Creek chiefs who signed a treaty ceding Creek land to the state of Georgia in February of 1825. His purported reason for doing so was that he understood that the white settlers would inevitably take the land anyway and believed it would be better for his people to sign the treaty and at least receive payment for what they were giving up. Unfortunately, his decision wasn't popular with everyone in the Creek nation. He was assassinated two months later in Carroll County by the Upper Creeks of Alabama.

Indian Springs Village enjoyed several peaceful decades during which it became a flourishing resort for wealthy folks from Atlanta wishing to escape the summer heat and partake of the waters. But that peace was shattered by the Civil War. In 1864 Sherman's right wing marched through this area. Two divisions were encamped at Indian Springs and Jackson while waiting to cross the Ocmulgee River.

We decided to drive into Jasper County to see just where the Federal Army was headed after crossing the river.

Indian Springs Hotel Museum

# Monticello

## JWW

Monticello was familiar territory for me because my in-laws, D.C. and Nan White, lived in Jasper County for a number of years. However, it was all new to Milam and she was taken with the picturesque farms and miles of rolling countryside.

As we approached Monticello (and that's pronounced *mont-ah-SELL-o* here in Georgia), the county seat, we took appreciative note of the beautifully restored homes lining the street. Then we were in the heart of town, which was built around a park-like square. At least it's called a square, even though it's really an octagon with uneven sides. We were looking for the marker observing the formation of the county and found it next to the courthouse north of the square.

Jasper County was created in 1807, but in the beginning it was called Randolph County to honor Virginia statesman John Randolph. However, it was just as easy to fall out of public favor in the early 1800s as it is today. Randolph opposed the country's entry into the War of 1812 and this offended the citizens of Georgia so much that the name of the county was changed to Jasper after Revolutionary War hero Sergeant Jasper.

As so often happens in politics, Randolph regained his stature in the state, probably with a show of repentance and heartfelt apology—the same approach that often works today. Anyway, the legislature later named another county for him and it still bears his name. The more things change...

We read the marker, then drove around the square and parked on the opposite side. We wanted a wide-angle view of the courthouse, the same view that attracted moviemakers when *My Cousin Vinny* was filmed here in 1992. That morning, I could almost see

Joe Pesci driving that big red Cadillac up to the front of the building.

We were in a Honda CR-V that admittedly didn't have the cache of a red Caddy, but it got us down the road in relative comfort. We left Monticello and drove south on Highway 11 through Adgateville and Hillsboro. Soon after passing into Jones County we came to Round Oak.

At first glance, it looked like any of the other little towns along the railroad track, but then we noticed the Ancestors' Memorial Garden. Built around what was once Miss Lily Gordon's store—which now functions as the Visitor/History Center—the garden honors the founders of the town. Designed by master gardeners using native plants and shrubs from local home places, it's a feast for the senses. Wind chimes sound softly in the breeze and the sun glints off the pane of a window, brightly painted and hanging from a tree. Old farm implements dot the landscape and stepping-stones engraved with the names of the honored ones are everywhere. What a wonderful way to celebrate ancestors.

As we continued down Highway 11, we passed Otis Redding Road and I remembered hearing that the legendary soul singer had been buried on his family's ranch in Jasper County.

We had an unremarkable lunch at a chain restaurant near Interstate 20, then headed home.

Jasper County Courthouse

# Sherman's Progress

## Monroe And Bibb Counties

In the fall of 1864, the right flank of Sherman's forces made its way southeast through Georgia. In Monroe County, on November 17, there was a skirmish on the north bank of the Towaliga River between Kilpatrick's Cavalry (US) and Wheeler's Cavalry (CSA). The Confederates burned the bridges across the river and stopped the Union Army's forward progress. Three days later, the Federal cavalry approached Macon, in Bibb County, from the east. They directed cannon fire toward the city from a high ridge near Dunlap Farm, but were repelled by Confederate forces. Eventually they continued southeast, leaving Macon relatively untouched.

# Forsyth

## MMP

Heading south on Interstate 75, we were on our way to Forsyth. Jackie was in the driver's seat arguing with herself about which way to turn once we exited the expressway. I was thumbing through notes about our day's plans, but my mind wasn't in gear. Putting down my folder, I started chatting.

"I like your blouse, Mrs. White."

"Thank you. I can only wear it when I'm away from home. See the feathers at the end of the tassels?"

"Yes, so cute."

"My crazy cat Spike is drawn to these feathers like catnip. The beast jumps out at me from every corner of my house. I never know when it will happen next. Spike thinks my blouse is his new toy."

"Maybe he believes you're morphing into a bird."

Today was my birthday. I wanted to spend time with Jackie, but research wasn't number one on my agenda. Fortunately, my thoughtful friend knows how to get me back on track.

"We're having lunch at the Whistle Stop Cafe in Juliette."

"Happy Birthday to me!" I picked up the folder and started enthusiastically reading about Monroe County, named for President James Monroe

The sunbaked February day provided yet another gift. It was oddly warm outside for midwinter, so we could do without coats. The sky was a brilliant blue. Birds chirped a welcome as Jackie snapped a photo of the Monroe County Courthouse. The stately building is surrounded by interesting shops and tempting restaurants. We took a walk around the town square.

The chimes on a nearby church welcomed the noon hour with a hymn.

"You won't hear this type of music in a big city."

"You're right. Listen, Jackie, listen to what's playing."

She began to sing along, "Dance, dance wherever you may be, for I am the Lord of the Dance, said he."

"Lovely, my friend."

Jackie reminded me "Lord of the Dance" was sung at the memorial service for her beloved Carl. A bird chirped. This was a sweet moment, indeed.

Getting back on task, we paused to admire a rather unique statue, a stunning tribute to Confederate volunteers. Of course, Jackie took a picture.

We stopped next at the historic marker, which salutes the gentleman for whom the town is named, John Forsyth.

Jackie giggled, "Milam, make a note. He is not the John Forsyth who starred in the television series *Dynasty*."

"Got it."

John Forsyth (1780-1841), a famous Georgia politician, was the U.S. Minister to Spain and served as the Secretary of State for two American presidents, Andrew Jackson and Martin Van Buren.

Another point of interest in the National Historic District of Forsyth is the old office of *The Monroe Advertiser*. From 1867 to 1870, long before he wrote the Uncle Remus stories, Joel Chandler Harris worked at the newspaper. During his three years there, he quickly rose from his job as a printer's devil to become an accomplished journalist. Harris's type-stand is still used in the present day office.

Although Forsyth's eateries beckoned to us, we stuck to our original plan for lunch at Whistle Stop Cafe.

# Juliette

## JWW

It was lunchtime and I'd promised Milam, who is the greatest movie fan I've ever known, a special birthday treat. Nearby Juliette, an unincorporated community named for the daughter of a railroad engineer, is located beside a railroad track and only a few hundred yards from the Ocmulgee River.

A number of movies have been filmed in Juliette since the 70s, but the most famous is 1991's *Fried Green Tomatoes*. We were going to have lunch in the cafe made famous in that movie. We settled into a high-backed wooden booth and gave our orders to waitress Victoria Wheeler.

The walls in the old wooden building were decorated with advertising signs and historic photos. The cafe was busy that Wednesday afternoon. While tourists like us occupied a few tables, most of the customers appeared to be local people – a good omen for the quality of the food. This proved to be true when Victoria set the fried green tomato salads in front of us. It only took one bite to know we'd ordered the right thing.

As we ate, we talked about the movie, recalling more scenes as they occurred to us. And we weren't the only ones. Four burly guys sitting in the booth behind us were also talking about the film. Judging from their clothes they probably worked in construction, and evidently one of the four had never seen *Fried Green Tomatoes*. His companions were delighting in telling him the story.

We couldn't hear everything that was said, but the last line came through loud and clear. "And they *ate* him!"

Back at our table, we'd finished the salads and our conversation also took a grisly turn.

"What was the name of the river we crossed coming here from Forsyth?" Milam asked. "Did you say something about scalping?"

"It was the Towaliga River and what I said was that the name means roasting scalp."

"Eeeuuu. Why would anyone call a river *that*?

So I told her what I'd learned in a book on the history of Middle Georgia. "Some Native American warriors used to take the scalps of their enemies as trophies. Naturally they wanted to be able to carry them home and show them off. Only problem was that rotting scalps smelled really bad."

Milam was growing more disgusted by the minute. "So they *cooked* them?"

"Yeah ... well, kinda. They dried them over a fire. You know how dried meat lasts longer? Sort of like jerky, I guess."

Milam put up a hand. "Please. No more."

"Well, you asked."

Milam clearly wasn't as interested in odd historical facts as I was.

*Note from Milam*: We didn't know it at the time, of course, but a few months later, Jackie, Jamey, and I would travel to Juliette. Yes, we'd again eat fried chicken and barbeque at the Whistle Stop Cafe. But the real excitement was that my husband and I got to watch Jackie's interview on a television program called *The Dead Files*. The show, featuring a policeman and a psychic, is a favorite guilty pleasure for us.

Donning her hat as a retired police officer and true crime writer, our multi-talented friend Jackie served as an expert witness on the reality show. Steve Di Schiavi, lead investigator for *The Dead Files*, questioned Jackie regarding her theories about a hit and run accident that had occurred decades back. Jackie, who isn't a big fan of ghost hunting, found the whole experience rather amusing, but did her job.

The star, Di Schiavi, a retired New York detective, said our friend was one of the best expert witnesses he'd had the pleasure of interviewing.

"I wish I could take her on the road with me," he said. "Jackie is a real pro."

I felt like a proud mother.

Milam and Jackie at Whistle Stop Cafe

# Macon

## JWW

The morning started with a very positive vibe. As soon as Milam was settled in the car beside me, I pushed the audio button and the insistent opening notes of "Midnight Rider" filled the air.

"We have a soundtrack for today's trip," I announced. We were headed for the middle Georgia town of Macon, which is synonymous with Southern music. "It's all Allman Brothers all the time. Just wish I had some Otis Redding and Little Richard, too."

"The Allman Brothers are fine." Milam had to raise her voice a bit to be heard. She didn't complain about the bumping percussion, but I turned the volume down to a level that allowed conversation.

"Jamey and I saw them back at the University of Alabama when they were the Allman Joys. They were great even then."

Content that I was in the company of another music lover, I relaxed and drove south.

Every March, Macon throws a ten-day party called the Cherry Blossom Festival. That Thursday fell right in the middle of the festivities. Even though only about half of the blooms had opened on the city's 300,000 Yoshino cherry trees, the celebration was in full swing. There were hot air balloon races, car shows, street parties, and nightly concerts in Central City Park. Many homes displayed pink wreaths on the doors, and mailboxes everywhere were festooned with bright pink ribbons.

We'd heard that they'd be giving away cherry ice cream in Third Street Park. It was tempting, but our time was limited, so we drove straight to the Otis Redding Memorial on Riverside Drive. There, high on the bank of the Ocmulgee River next to the Otis Redding Memorial Bridge, is a life-sized bronze sculpture of the legendary, late musician. He's sitting on bronze dock pilings, playing his guitar. There's a bronze writing pad beside him bearing the lyrics of "*Dock of the Bay.*" Just looking at him made me want to whistle the last notes of that song.

Next we drove to the corner of Middle Street and Fifth Avenue. It had probably been a nice, quiet neighborhood when the houses were built in the middle of the last century, but now the expressway runs right beside it. The modest frame house is Little Richard Pennington's birthplace.

After naming as many Little Richard hits as we could, we left downtown and headed north on Vineville Avenue. After a few miles we came to a big, Tudor-style house and drove through the open wrought-iron gates beside it.

From January of 1970 until 1973, the mansion was home to The Allman Brothers Band—along with an ever-changing cast of family, friends, and assorted roadies. Today it is The Allman Brothers Band Museum, where a dizzying collection of musical instruments, photos, films, posters, and memorabilia is on display. But perhaps the most extraordinary things a visitor finds there are the memories.

Docent Rex Dooley welcomed us warmly and gave us a personal tour of the place. We saw it all—the living quarters on the second floor, the gold-top guitar played on Eric Clapton's original recording of "Layla," and the kitchen where Dicky Betts introduced his fellow band members to a song he'd just written called "Ramblin' Man." Rex even took us up the stairs to the third floor landing to show us the stained glass window depicting the iconic mushroom.

We could have spent several more hours there, but we had a few more stops to make in Macon. So we got back in the car and followed the "Ain't But One Way Out" signs out of the parking lot and went on our way.

Rose Hill Cemetery spreads over sixty-five acres on the north bank of the Ocmulgee River. Opened in 1840, many prominent Maconites are buried here, including a governor, a senator, and several US representatives. It is also the final resting place of Allman Brothers Band members Duane Allman and Berry Oakley. They're buried side by side and the location attracts big numbers of fans every year. Ironically the cemetery was where the band hung out and wrote songs in the early days.

Before leaving the city, we had one more musical stop to make. The Allmans, Otis Redding, and Little Richard aren't the only famous musicians who hailed from Macon. Nearly a century before any of them took the stage, there was another who gained national prominence.

On High Street in the historic district is the cottage where Sidney Lanier was born in 1842. He was a remarkable man—a musician, poet, linguist, mathematician, and lawyer. Lanier was famous in his day as a flute player and composer. Now, however, he's better known as a poet, most famous for "The Song of the Chattahoochee" and "The Marshes of Glynn," a loving description of the marshes on the Georgia coast. Lake Lanier, northeast of Atlanta, was named in his honor.

Milam and Jackie at "The Big House"

Portrait of The Allman Brothers Band by Steve Penley

Sidney Lanier Cottage, Macon

Entrance to Rose Hill Cemetery, Macon

# Ocmulgee National Monument

## MMP

Who knew McDonald's offers salads? Nice surprise. After lunch, Jackie and I drove to the east side of Macon to the Ocmulgee National Monument. Finding our destination went smoothly because Jackie, a former Macon resident, knew exactly where to go.

"Dog violets," she exclaimed as we entered the park. "Love them!"

After admiring the field of tiny purple flowers, I looked across the road to our left and spotted the marker for Dunlap farm. It was here in late July of 1864 the Civil War Battle of Dunlap Hill was fought. Although Macon itself was never invaded, the Union forces did fire artillery at the city. An antebellum planter's town home, The Cannonball House on Mulberry Street, still bears the scar.

I could almost hear distant drums beating. Confederate soldiers? Union men? Neither. On the crisp March afternoon, my imagination's ghosts may not have been the specters of combatants in battle, but the spirits of the ancient people who lived on the Ocmulgee River plateau thousands and thousands of years ago. The land on which we stood has been inhabited continuously for seventeen thousand years.

Angela Bates of the National Park Service enthusiastically talked about the park's museum. A treasure trove of pottery, arrowheads, works of art, and jewelry, the building also houses colorful Native American costumes, along with sticks and balls used for sporting games many centuries in the past.

Angela was especially excited to show us one of the museum's greatest treasures. Pointing to an arrowhead, she announced, "Here we have the very first Clovis point ever found east of the Mississippi River! This find assures us the Clovis people were in this area."

Jackie and I wandered through the museum following a timeline beginning in 9000 BC with Paleo-Indians (Clovis) and progressing to the present day.

A basket filled with a mixture of clay and dirt caught Jackie's attention. The sign encourages visitors to lift it.

"This is what they used to build the mounds we'll be seeing." She attempted to pick it up. "Never mind, the thing's way too heavy for me!"

Apparently, Native Americans known as Mississippians would have been more determined than my friend as they carried load after load of the clay-dirt mixture on their backs to create the mounds. Each basket weighed between thirty and sixty pounds. We also learned that over the years the mounds were raised higher and higher as different leaders came into power. Like rings on old oaks, the layers of clay tell stories through a rainbow of earthen colors.

Leaving the museum, Jackie and I walked up to the most important mound in the park, a ceremonial council chamber dating from the Mississippian era.

Discovered in 1934 by archeologist Dr. A. R. Kelly, Ocmulgee's Earth Lodge is America's oldest ceremonial lodge. The chamber's clay floor has been carbon dated to 1015. We'd stepped back a thousand years in time.

Jackie and I ducked our heads and entered a circular room with fifty seats. In the center was a fire pit. We noticed the effigy of a bird, which is significant in many Native American cultures. It made us both think of Rock Eagle in Putnam County.

Visitors to the park are also offered inviting walking trails along with additional mounds. Atop one, a funeral mound, we enjoyed a terrific view of the Macon skyline with its magnificent church steeples, office buildings, historic homes, and Mercer University. Even at a distance, the striking pink colors of the city's annual Cherry Blossom Festival called us to take part.

Jackie checked her watch. Although there was much more to experience, it was well past time to leave. On the drive out of the park, she slowed her car by a historic marker referring to William Bartram (1739-1823), the famous explorer and diarist of flora, fauna, and Native American inhabitants.

"Ah ha, here's our connection with the present," I announced. Having experienced the Earth Lodge and archeological artifacts, the late 1700s seemed like recent history to us.

In 1775, Bartram wrote in his diary about "viewing Old Okmulgee fields," making note of "the power and grandeur of the ancients of the area."

The day was cool and a refreshing breeze sent us on our way. The sun shined as we left the park promising to return. Jackie had already brought her grandchildren to Ocmulgee National Park. I really want to bring our young boys, too!

Entrance to the ceremonial mound, Ocmulgee National Monument

Interior of the ceremonial chamber, Ocmulgee National Monument

# Sherman's Progress

## Baldwin County

On November 22, 1864, while the right wing of Sherman's Army was centered around Clinton and Gordon, the left wing arrived in Milledgeville. General Sherman and over 25,000 men camped on the east side of the city. They stayed there until November 25 when they marched on east towards Sandersville.

# Olive Forge

## MMP

It was 9:10 AM. My old Jeep's windshield wipers struggled to cut swift, but blurry glimpses through a dense, pounding rain. I gripped the steering wheel and prayed to dodge the thundering herd of 18-wheelers on I-285.

"Neither rain, nor sleet, nor dead of night," I mouthed, "shall keep me from my trip with Jackie today."

What were the post office people thinking when they penned such a threatening mission statement? I took comfort in knowing I was, at the very least, driving in the light of day. Twenty minutes later, I breathed a sigh of relief as I pulled into a parking space in front of our usual meeting spot, The Crossing restaurant located in the old train depot in Norcross. Located roughly halfway between our two homes, we'd started meeting here for lunch years ago when it was still the Norcross Station Cafe.

"Hop in," said Jackie, as she rolled down her window. "We're both crazy to drive in this."

"I'm just glad you're at the wheel." I clicked my seatbelt.

"Guess what? I'm taking you to Olive Forge today," she beamed. As if the weather were responding positively to Jackie's exciting announcement, the rain began to let up.

"Finally, I'll get to see it!"

I'd long yearned to visit her friends, Marsha and Darryl Herren, and tour their herb farm, which the two have lovingly designed and tended since 1972. Jackie frequently talked about the Herrens and their magical place.

What I didn't realize was the impact this brief stopover would have on me. It zeroed in on the character of our book. More than following Sherman's March to the Sea in search of historic markers, our book is about friendship, Jackie's and mine. This day, the Herrens would become the icing on the cake.

Admittedly, there is not a historic marker in front of Olive Forge. Not yet. But as we plan our stops, Jackie and I do tend to fudge just a little on the rules. Hey, it's our book!

In Haddock, Georgia, not too far from Milledgeville, Marsha and Darryl have created a magical seven-acre retreat, one which is filled with herbs and all things growing, along with a gift shop well stocked with herb-related products, homemade jellies, and unique works of art including stained glass creations by their son, Andy. Even in late winter, the grounds felt alive with the promise of spring.

As we made our way toward the herb farm, we stopped at historic Providence Baptist Church (1826) in Shadydale and wandered through the adjoining cemetery. I could almost hear the voices of those decades dead. The peacefulness of the experience soothed me. Rainclouds faded and light bathed the tombstones.

"Stress gone," I said.

"Just wait," said Jackie. "Spending an afternoon with the Herrens is as refreshing as a day at a spa."

She would prove herself right.

On cue, a rush of bright sunshine greeted us as we neared the turnoff onto Brown's Crossing Road. We drove up a gravel drive past the Herrens' pond and approached the property's main building, a welcoming and sturdy home, one that the couple built, board by board, completely by and for themselves.

"Come in!" greeted Marsha as she threw her arms around Jackie.

The sweet scent of lavender and other herbs filled the family room. A feeling of goodwill washed through my soul. Jackie had not exaggerated in the least. The Herrens' home was clearly a little piece of Heaven, and we'd not yet toured half of it.

My fledgling friendship with Jackie's friends was kick-started with a bang when Marsha offered us a treat.

"Petit fours," she said with a twinkle. "A friend brought these to us on Saturday.

"PETIT FOURS!" I squealed.

Jackie cut her eyes at me, obviously questioning my extreme burst of enthusiasm.

"Last night, I hosted my bridge club," I explained. "Not inspired, I ran by a bakery to pick up a cake or something, when a display of colorful petit fours caught my fancy. While preparing dessert for my friends, I salivated over those pastries. As the ladies played cards, I opened the bakery box. What! The clerk had shortchanged me by one bloomin' petit four.

"Crushed, I served the ladies. I put a scoop of ice cream on each plate, along with a few raspberries, and the darn petit four. Surely one of the girls would notice my barren plate and offer to share. But no."

Marsha grinned and gave me the pick of the pastries. Darryl hurried for his camera to capture my first bite. From that moment on, our friendship, like the herbs and plants in the Herrens' garden, took root.

We sat on their screened porch sipping tea as I learned more about this extraordinary twosome. Sweethearts for life, they've raised children and now enjoy their grandchildren and a great-grandchild. Along the way, they've counseled and they've taught. He's taken a turn as preacher and blacksmith, while she's mastered the garden and ultimately recruited him as fellow herb specialist. Marsha is quite the jelly-maker as well.

Her obviously proud husband remarked, "Marsha could make jelly from pond stones!"

Spending time with the two of them gives the visitor a rush of joy, a breath of healing air, an education, an appreciation of nature, a feeling of peace, and a sense that all is right with the world. I cannot wait to return.

Olive Forge is open to the public Thursday through Saturday.

Milam gets her *petit four*

Herren Home, Olive Garden Herb Farm

# Milledgeville
## (Part 1)

### MMP

A veteran Milledgeville tourist, I knew one day would only scratch the surface of one of Georgia's early state capitals, which was the political center of the state from 1807-1868. Jackie and I drove around admiring one stately mansion after another, when, absolutely starving to death, we hit pay dirt. We parked near The Brick, a place to gobble a yummy salad before heading out for our eagerly anticipated walking tour of Milledgeville.

After lunch, we picked up a map at the Welcome Center on Hancock Street. I shouldn't share this tidbit about our adventure, but I truly cannot help myself.

"The sign reads, 'Please use other door,'" said Jackie. "There must be another entrance. Let's go around to the side."

I was still preoccupied organizing my purse with cellphone, camera, notepad, etc. Like an obedient puppy, I dutifully followed her. Not finding the door, we wandered on to the back of the building. Oddly, there was still no place to enter.

"Ah ha, here we go," I said walking up a handicapped ramp . . . to a locked door!

I was having visions of an old *Twilight Zone*. Scratching our heads, Jackie and I returned to the main entrance.

"For heaven's sakes!"

"Please use other door" was clearly marked on the *left* side of a double glass door. Key word, DOUBLE.

Chuckling, I held the right one open for Jackie. She looked at me and burst out laughing. Once inside, we were nearly hysterical as we struggled to communicate with the young lady manning the information desk.

A professional oozing with Southern charm, she pointed to an array of brochures. In her hand was a cellphone, likely a protection device in case of crazed tourists like us. As in this piece, I had to share our funny misunderstanding with her.

"That is a first," she grinned, giving us a map and carefully and slowly, very slowly, going over directions for our walking tour. As we left the center, map and brochures in hand, she commented, "Wish I could go along with you. You two ladies could be a lot of fun."

"She thinks we're stupid," I said once we were outside.

"Or worse," Jackie said.

Our first stop was to be an early home of Flannery O'Connor.

"There it is," shouted one of us. I won't say who.

At that moment, my phone rang. It was one of my children calling. Thoughtfully, Jackie urged me to chat. As I was talking, I noticed Jackie had stopped a gentleman to confirm that we were, indeed, looking at the correct house.

When I caught up with her, Jackie was thanking the man. A bit flushed, she turned our map upside down. Make that right side up!

"It works better this way. There's the house," she cleared her throat, "across Greene Street."

The magnificent Cline-O'Connor-Florencourt House, circa 1820, took our breath away with its widow's walk and Ionic columns. From 1838 to 1839, the home at 311 West Green Street served as the governor's mansion.

From there, we enjoyed an easy stroll down tree-shaded sidewalks toward the Old Governor's Mansion on South Clarke Street. As we walked, I told my friend about another tour, one I took years and years ago in Milledgeville.

A couple of dear, darling, prouder than proud Southerners drove me around town to show me the sights for an upcoming magazine feature I was writing. We stopped, as I recall, at St. Stephen's

Episcopal Church where, they told me, Union horses had been stabled.

"Horses! Can you imagine!" frowned one of my guides.

According to the ladies, the horrid soldiers actually poured thick sorghum syrup into the church's fine pipe organ. In defense of those Yankee devils, after the war was over, an insurance firm in New York City replaced the organ. That part of the story, the ladies approved.

My favorite conversation between the delightful twosome involved a lovely neighborhood near Memory Hill Cemetery.

Glowing, one of the Southern belles began, "A fine Confederate soldier was hiding from the Yankees up in the attic of that very house."

Her friend interrupted. "No dear, it was the home across the street."

"Whatever. All the neighbors knew he was there. They helped the poor dear earn a little money by having him shine their shoes. Each night they'd leave their shoes on side porches. The courageous boy would creep out at dark, pick up the dirties, and, in timely fashion, deliver nicely shined shoes!"

"No, dear, I believe he was a Yankee deserter. He had *people* here."

"I KNOW he was one of ours," huffed belle number one.

Jackie and I stood in front of the Old Governor's Mansion, (1839, High Greek Revival) the home for Georgia governors from 1839 to 1868. To the dismay of many, it was occupied briefly by General Sherman. The structure was lovingly and beautifully restored during a three-year period beginning in 2001. A must-see in Milledgeville, the National Historic Landmark and museum is open to the public. My husband and I have had the pleasure of touring the mansion.

Back to the car, we found the Old State Capitol (1807, Gothic). According to our brochure, it is the finest example of Gothic architecture in a public building in the United States. The structure, now a museum, is the centerpiece for Georgia Military College. Sherman's soldiers occupied it for a while in 1864 and did considerable damage to the building. It has also survived two fires. Like the Governor's Mansion, the Old State Capitol has also been returned to its original grandeur.

Before leaving the area, we drove out of town to have a look at Central State Hospital. Jackie's book *Whisper to the Black Candle* (1999) tells the story of convicted murderer Anjette Lyles who spent many years in Georgia's notorious mental hospital. Today, however, it is just a collection of depressing, institutional block buildings that don't hint at its dark past. We didn't linger.

Checking the time, it was obvious a single day wasn't going to be enough for us to appreciate the wonders of Milledgeville, Georgia. Reluctantly driving toward home, we chatted over a couple of drive-through milkshakes from Dairy Queen.

"We'll come back to see more of Milledgeville," said Jackie.

"And Andalusia," I prompted, expressing our need to see the farm where Flannery O'Connor wrote so many of her incredible works. "After all, we're writers, too."

Double door, Milledgeville

Old Governor's Mansion, Milledgeville

# Milledgeville
## (Part 2)

### JWW

We went back to Milledgeville a couple of weeks later. I wasn't as familiar with the place as Milam, who was a regular visitor, but I did appreciate its historic charms. It's located right in the middle of the Antebellum Trail, which meanders through Georgia's Historic Heartland from Athens to Macon.

As a history buff, strolling the old district in the city was right up my alley. Our uncanny good luck with the weather held, too. Even though it was early April, we had blue skies, temperatures in the 70s and gentle breezes. It was as close to perfect as it could be.

We followed the tree-lined streets past big white houses with graceful columns framing front porches that invited you to sit and rock and pass the time of day. Flowers bloomed on the lawns of Georgia College and State University. And a few blocks away, we found Memory Hill Cemetery.

It was a fine day for the self-guided walking tour laid out in the brochure we'd picked up at the Visitors Center. We walked the narrow lanes past the final resting places of soldiers from every war, starting with the Revolution up to the present day. Buffalo soldiers, Confederate and Union men, and soldiers from both World Wars are all buried here.

We were left with the realization that death is the great equalizer. Renowned politicians and scientists share the hallowed ground with a notorious murderer. Plantation owners are buried near former slaves. The graves of the great lie beside folks known only to friends and family. There are even two dogs buried here—favored pets of Charles Bonner.

The Georgia Military College stands at the intersection of Jefferson Street and East Greene. Across from the school is a marker I'd been hoping to find. On this spot in 1807 John Clark horse-whipped Charles Tait.

No, it wasn't the result of a couple of rowdies in a drunken scuffle. These two men were prominent politicians and this was only one of several violent incidents that resulted from a decades-long feud.

John Clark, a Revolutionary War veteran and a member of the Georgia House of Representatives, was the leader of a state political faction mostly made up of emigrants from the Carolinas and settlers who had recently come to Georgia. William Harris Crawford and George Troup led the opposing faction of Virginia emigrants and established Georgia residents. It was a case of the aristocrats versus the common man.

In 1802 Crawford killed one of Clark's allies in a duel. Clark tried to return the favor when he and Crawford met on the "field of honor" four years later, but only succeeded in wounding his opponent. He tried challenging Crawford to a second duel, but the man intelligently refused.

Angered by the refusal, Clark turned his frustration on one of Crawford's supporters. He laid in wait for Judge Charles Tait on the streets of Milledgeville, cornered him and whipped him with a riding crop. Clark was summarily found guilty of the assault and fined two thousand dollars.

You'd think the public disgrace might have kept him from seeking office again. But if you believe that, you don't know politicians. Beginning in 1819, John Clark was elected to two two-year terms as governor and only missed a third term by six hundred votes.

I stood there on Jefferson Street and reflected that Clark would have fit comfortably in today's political arena. Some things never change.

# Andalusia

## MMP

We had, had, HAD to go to Andalusia. When Jackie and I toured Milledgeville, I kept insisting we visit the last home of Flannery O'Connor. Today we were finally on our way.

After battling Atlanta traffic and motoring east for nearly two hours, we turned off Highway 441 onto a gravel, tree-lined road and headed toward the nineteenth-century clapboard farmhouse. Sweet smells, lush greenery, blue sky with white puffy clouds, and inviting rocking chairs on the front porch called our names. A refreshing place, immediately both of us were filled with a sense of harmony.

I'd been to Andalusia twice before, but this visit was more significant, because I was there with my writing buddy. Jackie and I began our walk-about following in Flannery's very footsteps. We wandered around the grounds of the former dairy farm with its out buildings, the barn, a water tower, the milk house, and the old home of the Hill family, who'd worked the farm.

"We are walking through the pages of her stories," I whispered as if in a church. Flannery's characters seemed to peek out and wink at us from behind the big oak trees.

On a previous visit to the farm, I'd inquired about the famous peacocks of Andalusia. Long missing, I was told there was only a small possibility of bringing them back.

Flannery O'Connor was a bird lady of the first order and was known for her love of peacocks. She also raised ducks and chickens, along with flocks of geese and pheasants, and exotic birds such as ostriches, emus, and toucans.

Suddenly I noticed the large shelter where several of the birds perched. "The peacocks have returned!"

My enthusiasm grabbed Jackie. She, too, hurried behind me to snap pictures.

Later we learned Flannery's mother, Regina, did not share her daughter's fondness for the regal fowl. Not only were they loud, she had complained, but they also ate her flowers. Not to be undone, Regina planted beds of irises. It is the single flower peacocks will not eat.

As a side note, several years ago, I purchased a bag of Regina's iris bulbs. Thriving, its descendants currently grace my own garden.

Entering the O'Connor house, we were greeted by April Moon, the operations manager. She was all about Flannery and most knowledgeable about the author's work. April escorted us through the farmhouse and described Flannery's daily routine.

"She always attended daily Mass with her mother at Sacred Heart Church in Milledgeville," she began. "Afterwards, the two returned home so Flannery could write from nine to noon."

Jackie and I stood gazing into the study/bedroom with its original furnishings complete with knickknacks, including many bird objects. Sun shone in through the window as I tried to capture the image of Flannery's fingers on the keys of the old typewriter. Was she pounding out the words of "A Good Man is Hard to Find?" I felt the rush of a cool breeze.

"For lunch," added April Moon, "Regina often took Flannery to their favorite spot, The Sanford House."

Jackie and I shouted in unison, "We're there!"

"Sorry, but it's gone," lamented our guide. She added with a twinkle, "Flannery loved the Sanford House's peppermint chiffon pie. So, in honor of her birthday on March 25, I baked several chiffon pies."

It was obvious this young lady enjoyed her job. She mentioned that Flannery, who had a delicious sense of humor and had perfected the art of story telling, often entertained guests in the afternoons.

April pointed out the martini set placed atop the refrigerator. I found myself wishing Jackie and I could share a cocktail with Flannery on her front porch. Just imagine the conversations.

The truth be told, I'd be so star-struck by the presence of Flannery O'Connor, I would be chattering like a magpie. Did I say pie? Yes, and I'd be drooling peppermint chiffon down my double chin.

Our tour had started with a short informative video. We learned a bit more about Flannery's career, her early years in high school, and her life as a student at Milledgeville's Georgia College for Women, now Georgia College and State University. Not only could Flannery write incredibly well, but she was also an artist and gifted cartoonist for her school's various publications.

Additionally, we discovered Andalusia had been in Flannery's family for many years, and, as a child, the adventuresome little girl had galloped all about the farm on horseback.

After graduation, Flannery was invited to the prestigious Writers' Workshop at the University of Iowa. She then moved to Connecticut and New York in pursuit of her promising career. One of the most celebrated authors of the twentieth century, Flannery would publish two novels along with many essays and two dozen short stories.

Midway into her career, she received the devastating diagnosis of lupus, the same debilitating disease that claimed her father's life. Flannery returned to Georgia. In order to make her daughter as comfortable as possible, Regina moved from her Milledgeville home out to the Andalusia farm.

Flannery lived out her last thirteen years there, writing and enjoying her friends, both human and of the bird variety.

Flannery O'Connor died on August 3, 1964. She was only thirty-nine years old.

I arrived home around six o'clock that afternoon. I walked to my garden and noticed a purple iris newly in bloom, an offspring of its Andalusia kin.

"Well, hello, Regina. Today Jackie White and I enjoyed every moment at your farm. By the way, Flannery's peacocks are back."

Main house, Andalusia

Pond on the grounds, Andalusia

# Sherman's Progress

## Twiggs County

Bypassing Macon, Sherman's left wing headed toward Milledgeville. Confederate troops attempted to stop their progress at Griswoldville in Twiggs County on November 22, 1864. But the 1st Division, Georgia Militia was no match for Sherman's battlehardened troops. It's said that when Union soldiers returned to the battlefield after their victory, some broke down and cried when they saw the bodies and realized that the enemy force they'd defeated was primarily made up of young boys and old men.

# Geographic Center Of Georgia

## MMP

O ur first destination that March morning was to find the historic marker for the exact center of our state, supposedly located in Twiggs County. It's a complicated equation, but we'd planned to quickly find the marker and take a picture. Mission accomplished.

I was already in a questionable mood, because my eating buddy for the next three days had just announced that she had begun a diet. Not only that, but Jackie had already lost eight pounds! All I could do was support her. But how? By not eating anything fattening myself. Drat. When I agreed to work on this book with her, Jackie said we'd eat our way through Georgia. I believed "meat and three" was carved in stone. But now it would be "salad and unsweet tea." She's my friend. I signed on for the book, and now I'd signed on for OUR diet. We passed through Macon.

"Okay," Jackie said. "We're getting off at Exit 7."

The next thing I knew, we were at Exit 8. Doubling back not once but twice, we discovered there *was* no Exit 7. Again, we had entered the *Twilight Zone*.

Lately, things were not going well for our project. Mother Nature had already sabotaged our trip one time. Two weeks prior, a weather forecast of ice and snow cost us a $90 deposit at a Savannah bed and breakfast. This day, dreadful traffic had put us an hour behind schedule. Ever faithful, however, we continued on with our quest for the center of Georgia with road map, a list of historic markers, Jackie's carefully printed out directions, and a top notch GPS system in her car. We are not easily discouraged. We left the expressway and snaked along back roads for a while.

"There it is!"

"The marker!"

"Well, the marker for the dead town of Marion. The center of the state should be nearby."

"Dead town? Zombies?"

Jackie rolled her eyes. "A dead town is a once thriving community which voted against allowing trains to be routed through it. When that happened, the community usually lost the economic gamble and became a ghost town."

We read the marker. Interestingly, the community had once thrived nicely, serving as the first county seat of Twiggs County. Marion was named for Gen. Francis Marion, the Revolutionary hero known as the "Swamp Fox." But now there were only a few houses left.

Unfortunately, we never found the marker for the geographic center of Georgia. But as we motored through what was a most gorgeous landscape, we began to notice fields greening up, tulip trees showing off their large pink blooms, plums in blossom, and ornamental cherry trees.

We might not have found the center of Georgia, but we'd certainly come upon springtime. Jackie and I delighted in our morning and were as relaxed as the contented cows grazing in lush green fields.

We chatted about a popular TV reality show featuring two "pickers," men who travel the backroads of America looking for antiques, items considered by some as junk. Pickers recognize these finds as true treasures of Americana. The pickers would have been right at home on the roads we were traveling that day.

"Look out, turtle!" shouted Jackie. She swerved to miss the creature that was slowly crossing the road.

"Let's rescue him," I said.

She made a quick U-turn, our third of the day, not including the drive back toward Macon in search of Exit 7.

An 18-wheeler sped toward the turtle. "Noooo!" shrieked Jackie.

Miraculously, the truck missed him and the turtle cheated certain death. Jackie parked in the median. She carefully approached the box turtle, picked up the lucky little creature, and carried him to safety near water on the other side of the highway.

A man stopped to offer his assistance, thinking we'd broken down. She thanked him, explaining her actions.

He laughed, "Another turtle rescuer!"

We both felt mighty good about the turtle. Jackie named him "Sidetracked."

A few days after our trip, Jackie and I met for lunch.

"I've been vindicated," she announced handing me a road map. "There it is, just south of Macon. See? Exit 7!"

I looked at the map. She was right. Exit 7 was right there.

Jackie smiled only slightly. "Of course, the map's dated 1993, but a map is a map. Right?"

"Right."

"Who knew an exit could disappear?"

I sipped my tea.

"We never did find the geographic center of Georgia."

# Sherman's Progress

## Wilkinson County

In November of 1864, Sherman's right wing marched south via McDonough to Gordon. On the 24th, after the battle of Griswoldville, they moved on to Irwinton in Wilkinson County where they burned the courthouse and school before moving on.

# Wilkinson County

## JWW

Tuesday was a day filled with back roads and small towns. After our wild goose chase after the center of Georgia, we pointed the car east toward Wilkinson County. The mostly rural county, which has a population of around ten thousand, was created in 1803 and named for Revolutionary War General James Wilkinson. But a century before that an English trading post had been located here.

In the little town of Irwinton, the county seat, we found a small park-like area beside the county buildings and the marker we'd expected to find, commemorating the founding of the county. But there was more. Behind the marker was a stone pillar topped with what looked like a metal bowl. A fire burned in the bowl.

"An eternal flame?" Milam asked.

I leaned forward to read the Flame of Freedom plaque. "It was presented to the county by the American Legion in 1969, dedicated to all those who've served in the armed forces."

As we watched the flame dance in the cool breeze, it seemed a fitting tribute.

Minutes later, we were back on the country roads. Of course, we missed a turn or two and had to backtrack a bit, but it didn't seem to matter. All around us were fields and barns and early spring blooms.

"It's so pretty," I said. "Nothing is blooming at home yet."

Milam smiled. "You and I are going to have *two* springs this year. We can enjoy this one and then, in a couple of weeks, see it all over again in Atlanta."

We planned to have lunch in Sandersville that day, but there was a stop we wanted to make first.

Wilkinson County Courthouse, Irwinton

# Sherman's Progress

## Washington County

On November 25, 1864, Sherman and his troops came through Washington County. General Sherman set up headquarters in the Brown House in Sandersville. The army left two days later after burning the courthouse and jail. In Tennille, they destroyed the railroad tracks, depot, and water tank.

# Washington County

## JWW

"We're going to Washington County," I said, "place called Giles Crossroads. It's the site of a farm that's been in the same family for two hundred years."

Washington County, formed in 1784, is the only county in the US named for George Washington while he was still a general. As we traveled up Highway 272, we found more markers. Sherman's right wing passed this way near the intersection with what's now Highway 68. They'd crossed the Oconee River just to the west.

A couple of minutes later, after entering Washington County on Deepstep Road, a beautiful sight came into view. Tall and rustic and barn red, it sat close to the side of the road. A small sign hanging on the building identified it as O'Quinn's Mill, established in 1807 by Col. Thaddeus Holt. Just past the mill was a bridge over Bluff Creek, where the water rushed over the millrace, still ready to turn a grist wheel. I learned later that the colonel had also operated a ferry here.

It was such a pretty, peaceful place that we had to pull over and get out for a better look. A soft breeze came to us off the water and I could feel all the tension—the stress I'd built up as we'd fought our way through Atlanta traffic—melt away.

We strolled along the road back to the front of the building. The mill was shuttered and there was no one around.

"You'd think there'd be a marker here," I said, but we couldn't find one.

The yard held only a flagpole and an old cannon, green with age, a testament to old battles. We wandered back to the bridge.

"I could stay here all day," Milam said, then grinned. "If I wasn't starving."

My stomach rumbled at the thought of food and I realized that it had been a long time since breakfast.

"We'll find a place soon," I promised, "right after Giles Cross-roads."

Our next destination was only a couple of miles down the road where Indian Trail Road, a dirt road, entered Deepstep Road. Two markers stood at the intersection and from them we learned we were standing on the land settled by Alexander Giles in 1805. His descendants still live on the land. The Indian Trail Road marker was even more intriguing. For centuries, it had been a path along a high ridge used by the Creek Nation for their seasonal migrations. We were amazed at the history that must have unfolded here in what, today, is just a small, pastoral community on a Washington County backroad.

Fifteen minutes later, we arrived in Sandersville and found a Waffle House for our delayed lunch. Mindful of the diet I'd started, I ordered a grilled chicken salad. I was surprised that Milam did the same.

Then, happily full, we took a slow ride around the picturesque town. We'd planned to only drive through the streets in the historic district to see the lovely houses, but one—a green Victorian with serious-looking bars on the windows in the rear wing—caught our attention.

"That's odd," Milam said. She read the sign on the front lawn. "The Old Jail Museum and Genealogy Research Center."

Well, that was different enough to warrant a visit. We parked behind the old house and walked around to the front, passing the barred windows on the side. The museum was open. We walked in and were soon greeted by a charming woman who seemed surprised to have visitors all the way from metro Atlanta. She asked what brought us to Sandersville and we explained we were just passing through.

She laughed. "Most people have to be coming here to come here."

She showed us around the house. Located on Jones Street, it was built about 1891 and soon became the home of the sheriff. He and his family lived in the front section and the back became the jail. The cells, complete with the original locks, still remain. Visitors can even have a look at the padded one, reserved for out-of-control prisoners.

One thing we didn't see while we were there was Essie, the resident ghost, but tales of her presence are well known around Sandersville. In fact, a ghost-hunting team from South Carolina has spent several nights in the museum in the last few years, hoping to detect paranormal activity. I was sorry we missed Essie.

The Sandersville Jail was a natural lead-in to our next stop. We drove north from town, several miles to the community of Warthen. Soon after Washington County's formation, the general store. Warthen was chosen as the place for the country's first superior court sessions to be held.

While there's no trace of the court today, on a tiny side street we found the hewn-log jail, still standing after two hundred years.

"That's a *jail?*" Milam asked.

It was a reasonable question. Barely ten feet square, it looked more like a farm shed than a jail. But it did appear to be secure enough to keep someone prisoner. The logs were easily six feet wide and the heavy wooden door was secured with a chain and padlock. The padlock was new and I could only imagine what the original one must have looked like. Peering through the gaps between the logs, we could see only a dirt floor.

"What a horrible place to be locked up," I said.

The jail is notable not only for its age, but for its most famous prisoner. In 1806, Aaron Burr and a band of colonists had traveled south towards Louisiana. It was his intention to annex parts of Louisiana and Mexico to establish his own independent republic, a move the government of the United States wasn't about to approve.

So, in February of 1807, Burr was arrested in Alabama for treason. During the journey back to Richmond, the party stopped in Warthen and Burr was held for one night in the jail there. Later that year, he was tried in Richmond and acquitted.

O'Quinn's Mill

Old Jail Museum, Sandersville

Old Jail, Warthen

# Sherman's Progress

## Jefferson County

In late November of 1864, Federal troops marched into Louisville. The courthouse and several businesses on Broad Street were burned, and some private residences ransacked.

On the 28th, the 20th Corps destroyed the railroad from Davisboro to Spiers Turnout, then rejoined the main force in Louisville.

# Jefferson County

JWW

East of Sandersville, in Jefferson County, we found Louisville, one of the oldest towns in Georgia. In 1794, the coastal colonists moved to this location because they wanted to build their capital on higher ground, in a place with good drinking water. The town was chartered in 1786 and named in honor of King Louis XVI of France for the help he and his country gave to the colonists during the Revolution. In 1798, the Constitutional Convention was held here. And Louisville was the capital of Georgia until 1807.

The town was busy that afternoon, crowded with after-school traffic and shoppers. The large Jefferson County Courthouse is on US Highway 1, just outside the center of town, a massive structure set well back from the road. This present-day building is located on the site of the original Louisville courthouse.

After walking around the grounds for a few minutes, we made our way back to the middle of town. It was a pretty place.

"I always wanted to live in a small town," I said.

"Me, too. It must be wonderful to be able to walk to stores and restaurants and live where you know all your neighbors."

I agreed. "Guess it's too late for us."

"Afraid so."

It was a conversation we'd shared numerous times during our research for this book. We both found small towns attractive. But we knew no matter how much we romanticized living in one, our roots were sunk too deep where we were.

Jefferson County Courthouse

# Louisville Market House

## MMP

We stepped into Louisville's Market House. Built between 1795 and 1798, it was the center of commercial sales in Jefferson County. Because Louisville served as the State Capital of Georgia from 1794 to 1807, the square was a major transportation and commerce center.

Of great interest to us was the town bell. Cast in France in 1772, the bell was being shipped to a convent in New Orleans when pirates attacked and sacked the ship. Oh, but if this bell could only talk, the tales it could tell! Sold in Savannah, the bell found a new home in Louisville in the Market House, where, for decades, it rang out warning signals to the community.

I've tiptoed around "commercial sales." There was much commerce dealing with land and other properties, but the truth must be revealed. Slaves were also sold in the Market House.

My eyes lifted from the lovely bell to the original timbers of the centuries old structure, timbers that secured the roof just above our heads.

Slave market. We were standing in the middle of a slave market. Chills crawled up and down my back. I closed my eyes feeling the presence of men, women, and children, actual children, with their mothers and fathers, many of whom were being sold off and torn apart from one another. Families were being taken away to uncertain and possibly abhorrent situations. Most would never see one another again. Some would die.

Could it be that the heartbreak of these anguished souls is trapped in those ancient wooden beams? I believe them to be in a sacred, safe place now. Even so, does their heartache linger to remind us of the shameful past?

Almost sickened, I took a breath. Jackie urged me back to her car.

A sound. Church chimes. A hymn. Louisville United Methodist Church was before us. Its gentle chimes lifted my heart. Sun gleamed through stained glass windows. Angels appeared. I felt comforted.

Louisville Market House

Bell at Louisville Market House

# Bartow

## MMP

Our weather was absolute perfection. The tranquility of the Georgia countryside called to us, "Relax, enjoy." In pecan orchards, every tree stood sentry, as it seemed to offer peace and order along our afternoon's journey.

"Each pecan tree is lined up perfectly," I observed.

Jackie recalled her husband Carl telling her a story about one of his maternal ancestors, William Baugh. Baugh lived in Gwinnett County in the mid 1800s. He was a very particular man. Once when he was planting an orchard, he hired a neighbor to help. Baugh demanded that the saplings be in perfect alignment. If even a small twig of a tree was as much as a couple of inches off, he insisted that his helper dig it up and replant it in the correct spot. After replanting one tree four times and never locating it to Baugh's satisfaction, the neighbor quit and vowed he'd never work for him again.

Such perfectionists must have planted every grove we passed. All the trees were lined up as if they were soldiers standing tall in formation.

Jackie humored me by taking a detour to Bartow. I wanted to show her Charlton Hall (circa: 1917), the second home of our next-door neighbors and longtime friends, the Brantleys. Were one to look in the dictionary under "Southern," it's possible this couple's picture would appear.

Mary Charlton Evans Brantley, who grew up in Bartow, is the great-great granddaughter of Col. Beverly Daniel Evans, CSA, a veteran of the battle of Griswoldville.

As we approached the small town, we passed inviting pastures awash with daffodils. The carpet of yellow seemed to go on forever.

"My favorite flower," I commented.

"Mine, too."

Thanks to her late mother, my co-author is quite knowledgeable about growing things. In fact, I must put in a plug for her book, *A Southern Woman's Guide to Herbs.* (Mercer University Press)

"Those daffodils have naturalized," Jackie explained. "The old home places may be long gone, but certain flowers, including daffodils and daylilies, will come back year after year and spread all over the place."

"That's kind of sad," I lamented. "It's almost as if they return looking for their people."

Jackie thinks I take some things a bit too much to heart. On we drove as the sun glistened on the unusually warm spring afternoon. Cows mooed. Goats scampered about as chickens scattered.

We entered Bartow.

"Check out that gorgeous home!" said Jackie, slowing to take a closer look.

"That's Charlton Hall," I beamed.

I pointed out the playhouse in the back yard. A young Mary Charlton Evans sweetly wiled away hours in her miniature home, complete with electricity. Five grandchildren have delighted in making mud pies and leaf pancakes in their "Mimi's" childhood haven.

Quite often, Mary and Marvin Brantley entertain family and friends in Bartow. A safe place to play, children can roam freely down the street past the churches to explore a row of wonderful old buildings, which once served as the bank, post office—complete with the original post boxes—and, of course, Bryant's, Inc.

In 1919, Mary's beloved grandfather, Charlton S. Bryant, along with his wife, Mary Speir Bryant founded Bryant's, Inc. This building remains the headquarters for Mary's late brother Fred Evans's cotton and farming business, which is now run by his children, Rob Evans, Mel Kirk, and Lee Evans. Just recently Rob oversaw the renovation of a mule barn, located behind Bryant's near the ramshackled blacksmith's shop. The barn is said to be the oldest structure in Bartow.

Mary lights up when she shares memories of her grandfather's store.

"An old potbellied stove kept warm the area which held items including everything from ladies' fashions, men's and children's clothing, groceries, and pots and pans to tools, school supplies, and delicious hard candy."

She recalls her mother, Julia Bryant Evans, warning her of the dangers of touching the red-hot stove. "Mary Charlton, you could lose your fingers!" And listen the curious little lady did.

She also remembers her mother's exciting stories about the lady from Regenstein's Department Store in Atlanta, who periodically rode the train down to Bartow, bringing hatboxes with the very latest in millinery style.

"My mother loved hats until the day she died!"

During his visits to Bartow as a child, the Brantleys' son, Bryant, giggled at seeing his very own name around his mother's hometown. An advertisement, "Bryant's Gin" is still painted on the town's water tower.

Mary laughs. "Many a Yankee traveler stopped in Bartow wanting to buy a bottle of gin. They were disappointed to learn the ad was for my father Fred Evans's Cotton Gin!"

The Bartow Railroad station, the second oldest remaining station in Georgia, has been converted into the community's museum. The driving forces behind the museum were Hubert F. Jordan, his late wife, Patsy, and their two sons, Hubert and Todd. Among the many fascinating things a tourist will discover there is that the town was originally called "Spier's Turnout." The thriving community of farmers was the single stop between Macon and Savannah, the only one where two trains could pass; hence, "turnout."

On our brief trip through Bartow, we were surprised to find a historical marker there. It described the destruction of the railroad at Spier's Turnout by Federal troops in late 1864.

The name was changed after Gen. Francis S. Bartow, en route to Atlanta to fight for the Confederacy, addressed the citizens from the back of his train. Gen. Bartow is known throughout Georgia. His statue stands in Forsyth Park in Savannah, and Bartow County is also named for him.

A special memory Jamey and I have of Mary's hometown occurred many years ago when her mother passed away. A lovely funeral was held in the parlor of the Evanses' home. After the ceremony, the mourners walked out the front door following Mrs. Evans's coffin in a procession down the tree-lined street to the cemetery. It felt so peaceful, so Southern, and so appropriate. Miss Julia, the family matriarch, was laid to rest surrounded by her family, both the living and the dead.

Near her grave are two Confederate soldiers, 2nd Lt. John F. Spier, who was killed August 30, 1862 at the Battle of Manassas, and his brother, Dr. William A. Spier, who died at the Battle of Chancellorsville on May 3, 1863.

A black servant had accompanied the young brothers to war. When John was killed, his devoted slave buried him, carefully marking the location so he could return for his body. When the second brother died, the dutiful servant brought each young man all the way home in a mule-drawn wagon. Not only does this paint a heart-wrenching picture, but it also demonstrates the man's sincere dedication to the Spier family.

Bartow also has a theater, not a place where movies are shown, but an honest to goodness theater with actors who put on plays four times a year. The School House Players are folks from all around the area, old and young, who perform and direct, and also build scenery and make costumes for their productions. The theater is the all-consuming passion of home grown Bartowian, Charles Josey.

Mary Brantley could only talk to me for a minute more. She and Marvin were headed to Bartow with a couple of their Atlanta friends to see Josey's newest play, *"Bee's Business,"* based on a novel by Ann Cobb. Other upcoming productions include *"Cinderella,"*

"*Pump Boys and Dinettes*," and an eagerly anticipated Christmas Spectacular.

Mary wanted me to stress that all the plays are appropriate for every age. She added, "And have universal appeal."

Bartow feels like a step back in time. It's home, it's friendly. It is peppered with rich tradition and salted with treasured history. Bartow keeps on blossoming, just like those daffodils that adorn Georgia's spring pastures.

The big difference is that Bartow still holds on to its people. It's not unlike many small Georgia towns, I suppose. But I've been blessed to visit this one.

Depot Museum, Bartow, Courtesy of Todd Jordan

Young Mary Charlton at Charlton Hall, Courtesy of Mary Charlton Brantley

# Sherman's Progress

## Burke County

On December 4, 1864, Federal infantry brigades destroyed the bridges over Brier Creek, north and east of Waynesboro. They also fought skirmishes with Confederate defenders south of town and at Thomas' Station.

# BURKE COUNTY

## JWW

For our first night on the road, we chose Waynesboro in Burke County, mainly because the town was large enough to have several hotels. We checked in around 3:30, got settled in our rooms, then met back in the lobby.

"Let's drive around town, maybe find something interesting," Milam suggested.

"Okay with me. The only thing on our schedule for the rest of the day is dinner."

Something interesting? I'm embarrassed to say I hadn't done my research on Burke County. The only thing I knew was that Waynesboro was the county seat. Boy, was I in for an educational afternoon.

We found a parking space near the courthouse on Liberty Street and set out for a leisurely stroll around town. That's when we noticed the historic markers—they seemed to be everywhere. As we wandered from one to the next, we began learning about Burke County.

This area was settled early in Georgia's history. In 1758, it was organized as St. George's Parish. Some twenty years later it became Burke County, named in honor of Edmund Burke, an Irish member of Parliament and a staunch defender of the cause of the Georgia colonists.

I was still making notes on the creation of the county when Milam wandered over to another marker. She said something to me, but about that time a huge truck passed on the busy street. I couldn't hear a word.

"Wait a minute! I can't hear you."

I joined her beside the marker and she turned to me with a big grin on her face.

"You won't believe it! George Washington slept here! He really did!"

I sure hadn't seen that one coming. We read the words on the marker and learned that on his southern tour in 1791, President George Washington stopped here on May 17. He was traveling from Savannah to Augusta, but insisted on making a six-mile detour to visit Waynesboro, the community named for General Anthony Wayne. Washington had served with Wayne during the Revolutionary War.

The President spent the night in a house on Liberty Street, the street where we now stood.

"Washington sure wouldn't recognize the place today," I said, watching the busy scene around us.

We'd finished our tour of the square and started back to the car when Milam pointed to one of the banners adorning the street light poles.

"How does a town get to be the Bird Dog Capital of the World?" she asked.

I had no answer. "Maybe we'll find out while we're here."

The desk clerk at the Best Western recommended several places that we might try for dinner, including the Lakeview Restaurant.

"There's a lake here?" Milam asked.

"Yeah, right in town."

We found the Lakeview Restaurant just where she said it would be, on Liberty Street just a little south of the courthouse. Two minutes later, we were seated in one of the two dining rooms, looking out as the sun set over the lake. It seemed to be a small lake, but it was a lake nonetheless.

My resolve to stay on the diet didn't last long. The restaurant specialized in southern cooking, with an emphasis on fried seafood, so that's just what we had. My shrimp were delicious and very fresh—just what you'd hope for less than an hour from the coast. As our server, a friendly young man, filled our glasses, I asked him a question.

"Why is Waynesboro called the Bird Dog Capital of the World?"

"Guess it's because they hold so many field trials here, for the hunting dogs."

As we were paying our checks at the front counter, I noticed a concrete statue of a bird dog in the corner. It was painted with what appeared to be scenes from around town. I asked the cashier about it.

"Oh, those things are all over town. It was a school art project, I think."

I took a picture of the dog before we left.

We were walking back to the car when I saw yet another historic marker on the far edge of the parking lot. Of course, we had to go check it out.

The sun had set over an hour before, so I used the flashlight on my phone to illuminate the writing on the marker.

"The Old Quaker Road!" I said. "I've heard about this."

In the mid 1700s, it was one of the Province of Georgia's earliest vehicular highways. It led from Savannah to a Quaker settlement near present-day Wrightsboro in Columbia County. The thoroughfare is still in use today, but it bears little resemblance to the wagon road it was 250 years ago. In Waynesboro, it's a major road.

Burke County Courthouse

Bird dog statue, Waynesboro

# Shell Bluff

## MMP

Tuesday night, as we enjoyed perfectly fried shrimp beside a sunset-blessed view of a quiet pond in Waynesboro, Jackie and I began to relax. We congratulated ourselves for persevering long enough to locate three or four interesting historic sites for *Sidetracked*. So successful had we been during the afternoon, I actually considered the idea that our book's title no longer applied.

We discussed our agenda for the next day. Our first destination was a place called Shell Bluff. On the way to dinner that evening, we'd even seen a directional sign that read, "Shell Bluff." All we'd have to do the next morning was turn left at the courthouse and head to the fossil-laden spot.

Famed naturalist William Bartram, who traveled throughout Georgia in the mid 1770s, described Shell Bluff in his journal: "mammoth oyster shells jutting out along the Savannah River."

Intrigued by prehistoric times, I couldn't wait to explore the bluff. As we left the hotel the next morning, we drove back to the courthouse and turned left at the Shell Bluff sign.

I opened my file about Ocmulgee National Monument, the ancient Native American dwelling place we'd already visited, just across the Ocmulgee River from Macon.

"Ah ha, Jackie, I'd bet Bartram came to Shell Bluff on his way from Savannah to Ocmulgee."

She drove on smiling smugly. My co-author had finally gotten me hooked on doing research.

"Think about it," I began. "Two hundred and twenty-two years ago, Bartram traveled on horseback, camped, made precise notes, collected samples, and beautifully drew the native flora and fauna."

Jackie laughed. "And we're challenged simply trying to drive and find hotels!"

We drove for over half an hour.

"So how long until we get there?"

"Key phrase," replied Jackie, "Get there. Let's not count our chickens before they hatch. Don't forget our trying to find the geographic center of Georgia."

"That's just it. The bad stuff's over."

"Uh huh."

My enthusiasm was driving Jackie crazy. Ever optimistic, I almost expected the Native Americans of Shell Bluff to greet us astride wooly mastodons.

We turned onto a bumpy road, which seemed to go on forever.

A curious looking older gentleman, who was riding on a scooter, eyed us suspiciously. "Is he the mailman?"

"Don't think so. Going too slow and he doesn't seem to have any mail with him."

Apparently, the fellow was handing out flyers. I wondered if he knew where we might find Shell Bluff. Just then Jackie came to a sudden halt.

"What? Dead end!"

To our right was a gated community. To our left was a hunting club. We turned into the club drive. We could see a group of men inside. Bearded, apparently eating breakfast, they glared with disdain at us female intruders.

"Hunters have guns," announced Jackie. "Better back up."

She pointed out a steep, grassy bluff to our right, but hardly slowed up as we quickly exited the parking area. "I just hope that wasn't it," she said. "Too steep for me to climb and certainly not in these shoes!"

We passed the guy on the scooter. "Want to ask him?"

"NO!"

Taking the next left turn, I pointed out that we could see the Savannah River in the distance.

"That's a good sign," I chirped. "Where there's a river, there should be a bluff."

We headed toward Millen by way of Girard on Highway 23. The GPS suggested we turn right which seemed wrong. Nonetheless, we obeyed the authoritative female voice and made another turn, then another. After completing a full thirty-mile circle, we passed Plant Vogtle for possibly the third time. I'd lost count.

Bottom line: unlike Bartram, we quit.

Jackie suggested later that I contact the Chamber of Commerce in Waynesboro. Once back home with clothes in the washing machine, I made the call. A helpful young lady named Stephanie Folker agreed to help me.

"Oh yes," she said. "Daddy worked at Plant Vogtle. When I was a teenager, he would take me there to see Shell Bluff."

"Plant Vogtle, you say?"

"Yes, Plant Vogtle. I'd pick up fossils, shells, and all kinds of treasures. It was cool."

Plant Vogtle rang in my ears. All Jackie and I had had to do was turn LEFT. I laughed.

Stephanie said it might take her a little while, but she offered to do some research for us. I thanked her.

William Bartram was certainly a better explorer than we were. But then he didn't have the dreadful GPS woman misleading him.

Stephanie turned out to be a gem! A couple of days later, she emailed me pictures of the bluff, which included a close-up of fossilized shells. We give credit to her father, Tommy Oglesby. Over the weekend, he kindly went out to Plant Vogtle to take the photos for us. He even picked up a shell for me to keep as a souvenir.

Jackie and I must plan a return trip to Waynesboro, perhaps for a book signing!

In a follow-up email, Stephanie wrote, "Some of the better areas for viewing Shell Bluff are on private land and are difficult to get to by car."

Jackie and I feel totally redeemed.

Fossilized oyster shells at Shell Bluff, Courtesy of Tommy Oglesby

# A Phantom Plantation

## JWW

Our streak of bad luck continued that morning. After the Shell Bluff adventure, we took a side trip from Waynesboro in search of an antebellum plantation I'd read about. Unfortunately, even with directions straight from the historic marker website, we couldn't find it. We saw backroads, farmland, and fields that still bore the remnants of last year's cotton harvest, but no plantation.

We finally gave up and drove to Sylvania in Screven County for lunch. We might not have found the plantation, but we had our priorities straight.

# Sherman's Progress

## Screven County

Federal troops entered Screven County on December 4, 1864. Kilpatrick's Cavalry passed through Sylvania. On the 5th, while the 14th Corps camped at Jacksonboro, Sherman reached Oliver and set up his headquarters in a private home near the depot. He stayed there for four days, planning his army's next moves.

# Screven County

## JWW

Sylvania was another town we knew we could fall in love with, but we weren't there long enough to form a real attachment. After tuna subs, the diet a distant memory, we went back to work.

"What if we can't find anything else on our list?" Milam asked. "It's like we're cursed."

"We just had a couple of mishaps," I said with more confidence than I felt. "It's not going to happen again."

"What are we looking for this time?"

"Jacksonboro. It was the county seat of Screven County in the late 1700s. But now it's considered a ghost town."

"Sounds like fun," she said doubtfully.

When we reached the intersection of US 301 and Georgia Highway 24, five miles north of Sylvania, we found several historic markers lined up, one behind the other, on the road. We pulled to the side, parked, and went to check them out.

The first marker commemorated the establishment of Jacksonboro (which was spelled Jacksonborough at the time) in 1797. For fifty years, we learned, it had been a thriving commercial center for the area.

The second marker told the story of Dow's Bridge. In 1821 Leonard Dow, an itinerant preacher, had come to Jacksonboro. He wasn't pleased with what he found there and preached a fiery sermon condemning the population for their wickedness. Then, I'd learned from some additional research I'd done, Dow entered a tavern and, using an ax or some similar tool, destroyed a whole barrel of whiskey.

"Bet that made them mad," Milam said.

"Oh, yeah. They ran him out of town. He finally found refuge in the home of Seaborn Goodall. The legend says that, before leaving town, he stood on a bridge and cursed Jacksonboro, but asked God to bless Seaborn Goodall."

Over the next two decades, most of the homes and businesses in town were destroyed by mysterious fires, gusting winds, and flash floods. By the time Sherman's army passed through, there was little for them to destroy. However, one place remained untouched by storm, fire, and war—Seaborn Goodall's house.

"Well, it's an interesting story," I said, surveying the highway, which was empty of any traffic. "At least we found the markers. Just wish there was something more to see."

"I think there is." Milam pointed to her right down a sandy, unpaved road that ran off the highway. Beside it was a sign that read *The Dell-Goodall House, Brier Creek Daughters of the American Revolution*. And in the distance, half hidden by moss-draped trees, stood the old house.

We took the short walk down the road to the house. We couldn't enter the grounds because a high, chain-link fence surrounded the property, but we could stand there and admire the old place. We later learned that back in the 1960s the DAR had raised more than forty thousand dollars for the restoration of the house. Nowadays it's open for tours on special occasions.

"Do you think there really was a curse?" Milam asked.

I looked around us. "I don't know, but there's no sign of Jacksonboro, is there?"

Dell-Goodall House

# Sherman's Progress

## Effingham And Chatham Counties

On December 8, 1864, Sherman's right wing had reached Eden in Effingham County while his left wing was at Springfield. The following day, the army moved forward toward Savannah.

On December 13, Fort McAllister (CSA) fell to Union troops and Savannah was evacuated. On December 21, Savannah fell and Sherman and his army occupied the city.

# Effingham and Chatham Counties

## JWW

We drove from Sylvania to Savannah, through the small towns of Kildare, Shawnee, and Springfield. A side trip out of Springfield on Highway 275 brought us to a marker showing the area where two historic taverns had been located. And we learned George Washington spent a night here on his southern tour in the home of a man named Spencer.

"He really got around," Milam said with a chuckle.

Soon we were back on the road and, in a short time, driving into Savannah.

# Mother Mathilda Beasley

## MMP

As Jackie drove toward Savannah, I was getting very excited. The city holds many pleasant memories for me. Not the least of which is the 1999 wedding of our son, William and his beautiful wife, Abigail, in Whitefield Chapel (circa: 1925) on the campus of historic Bethesda School for Boys. Evangelist George Whitefield founded the original orphanage in 1740.

The present day school, now Bethesda Academy, is still located on six hundred acres on the banks of Moon River. Readers may remember *Moon River*, the hauntingly beautiful song written by native son, Johnny Mercer, the world-renowned lyricist, songwriter, and singer.

I digress.

Again.

Savannah is a mecca for tourism. Rare is the traveler who doesn't want to step back in history to walk the streets of the city founded in 1733 by James Oglethorpe. People yearn to enjoy River Street, tour square after square of gorgeous Victorian homes, including that of Juliette Gordon Low, founder of the Girl Scouts of America, take rides in buggies, peddle bicycles down brick streets, visit churches and museums, or follow the path of THE book, *Midnight in the Garden of Good and Evil*.

Part of our mission in writing our book has been to seek out lesser-known historic places along Sherman's March to the Sea. Jackie, in her ongoing quest to challenge me, suggested I do additional research about Mother Mathilda Taylor Beasley.

"I'm on it."

Born in New Orleans in 1834, it has been suggested that Mathilda possibly spent time in a Catholic orphanage following the death of her mother. Mathilda, a woman of color, came to Savannah as a young woman with a passion to teach black children in her home. Prior to the Civil War, what she was doing was a crime. This did not hold back the determined Creole woman.

Her life eventually took a turn for the better, when, in 1869, she married Abraham Beasley, a successful black businessman. Sadly, however, her husband passed away only eight years later.

Less than a decade after his death, Mathilda's devotion to black children's education along with her lifelong Catholic faith took her to York, England. There she studied to become a Franciscan nun as a member of the Poor Clare order.

The following year, Sister Mathilda returned to Savannah, where she started an orphanage. It would become the St. Francis Home in 1892. Notably, in 1889, she founded the first group of black nuns in Georgia. Mother Mathilda would work with her fellow sisters and with the beloved children until 1901.

Upon retirement, the dedicated nun lived in a small cottage on the property of Sacred Heart Catholic Church on Bull Street. Having donated all of her husband's landholdings to the church, she spent her later years sewing and using the money she earned to assist the poor black people of Savannah.

I stood transfixed reading the historic marker in front of Sacred Heart and marveled at the faith, strength, and resilience of this woman. Organ music drifted from the inside the church. I welled up in tears as I read of her death.

Just before Christmas in 1903, Mother Beasley was found dead, still kneeling in her cottage's private chapel. Always the organizer, the dutiful Catholic sister had laid out her clothes for burial. Beside her body was a will with instructions for her funeral.

Catholic and Protestant alike, black and white, the mourners completely filled the church for her funeral Mass. Typical of the beloved nun, no eulogy was permitted.

She is buried in the Catholic Cemetery on Wheaton Street.

In 2004, at a ceremony at Wesleyan College in Macon, Mother Mathilda was honored as a Georgia Woman of Achievement. In 2005, the Georgia Historical Society named Mother Mathilda Beasley as its Georgia Heritage Celebration Honoree.

Having read her story, I have to wonder if the remarkable nun is "planning" some way for her various awards to benefit those children who, like herself, continue to face so many difficulties in life.

One highlight of writing this book with Jackie has been becoming acquainted with Mother Mathilda.

Mother Mathilda marker, Sacred Heart

# Savannah's Squares

## JWW

Now it was time to see some of the historic places located in and around Savannah's famous squares. Readers might be surprised to learn that I sometimes overplan. Well, maybe you wouldn't. But that day was a good example of my doing just that.

I've been a frequent visitor to Savannah. Planning our itinerary for this trip, I remembered how congested the historic district was and how confusing driving around those squares could be. So I printed out a map of the area, highlighting our route. Then, taking note of the squares and the numerous one-way streets, I wrote meticulous directions to every separate location we were going to visit.

The way I figured it, I would drive while Milam read the directions aloud. For example, we'd drive down Abercorn, approaching Reynolds Square.

*Milam would say, "Turn right" and I would. Then she'd say "Turn left." I would. Then she'd say, "Turn left again" and I'd follow that command. Finally, she'd say, "Turn right on St. Julian and drive one block to the Johnson Square marker." And we'd be there.*

Simple, right? Not exactly.

As we traveled Abercorn, I said, "Okay. We're coming up on Reynolds Square. Read me the directions."

She consulted the paper in her hand. "Here it is. Reynolds Square. Turn right, left, left, left and right," she rattled off. "Oh, look at that house. Isn't it gorgeous?"

Of course, I was still making the first turn and had no idea what to do next. Too much information isn't necessarily a good thing.

But we muddled through, negotiating one-way streets, dodging tourists on bicycles, and managing to avoid oblivious pedestrians. The city was crowded with tourists, even on a Wednesday afternoon. We realized that St. Patrick's Day—Savannah's huge annual celebration—was only a week away. It looked like some people were getting an early start.

That afternoon was a marathon sightseeing trip for us. In addition to Reynolds Square, we saw Johnson Square where in 1735 Chekilli, Chief of the Creek Nation, recited the origin myth of the Creeks. We saw the church on Habersham Street where James Pierpont, the composer of *Jingle Bells*, served as music director in the 1850s. On Abercorn, we saw the marker honoring John Wesley's founding of his Methodist ministry in Georgia and one denoting the location of the parsonage where he resided in 1736.

Savannah is the site of the oldest congregation in the United States now practicing Reform Judaism. Congregation Mickve Israel was founded in 1733. They worshipped in various locations around the city until they built their own synagogue in 1790. We found the marker of that location at Bull and East Taylor Streets.

We parked the car and spent a while wandering around the Colonial Park Cemetery where the city buried its dead from 1750 until 1853. Many of Georgia's most distinguished citizens were buried here. Although Colonial Park was closed to additional burials in 1853 and no Confederate soldiers are buried there, the war still left its mark on the cemetery. Federal troops took over the place, looting graves and desecrating headstones. Today, Colonial Park is a city park as well as a historic site.

By 4:00, we'd both had as much history as we could stand. We drove the few blocks to our hotel on Bay Street. When I parked and took the key out of the ignition, I was ready to collapse. I felt like I'd been driving for a week and I'm sure sitting in the passenger seat hadn't been any easier for Milam.

"I'm not getting back in this car until we leave town tomorrow," I told her. "We'll have to walk to wherever we eat tonight."

She smiled. "That's okay with me. It's a beautiful afternoon."

She was right about that. The day was bright and sunny and, even though it was only March, the temperature was nearing 80 degrees.

"We've been blessed with good weather the whole time we've been working on this book. The only day it rained was when we went to the herb farm and, even then, the sun came out as soon as we got there."

Feeling decidedly fortunate, we checked in the hotel and found our rooms. It was only 4:30 when we left the hotel, this time on foot. It was too early for dinner, but I thought there might be a few more things to see.

"More history?" Milam asked.

"Well, this *is* where Georgia began."

She nodded. "You're right. We can't leave that out."

The historic markers were thick on the ground along Bay Street. We walked along Factors Row where we saw the old Cotton Exchange. We found a marker commemorating Oglethorpe's landing and the founding of the colony in 1733. We passed another at the Old City Exchange Bell that rang in the 1800s to signal closing time for the shops. It was also used by watchmen to alert citizens to fires and other emergencies.

We found our last historic marker in Savannah—in fact our last historic marker of the book—a few blocks farther down Bay Street in Emmet Park. The small park, about three blocks long, was once known as the Strand and later as Irish Green because it was so close to the Old Fort neighborhood where many of the city's Irish lived.

In 1902 the park was renamed in honor of Irish patriot Robert Emmet. That evening as the sun dropped behind the trees and the air cooled, we joined other people in the park. Couples strolled hand in hand, children shouted and frolicked.

"This is the perfect place to end our book," I declared.

Milam gave me a happy smile. "Perfect," she agreed. "Let's take a walk along the river."

We followed a steep cobblestone drive down to River Street. Standing there, with the river making its slow, heavy way past us, we finally relaxed. We'd found the destinations we'd set for ourselves—well, most of them anyway. We'd had some great experiences and, best of all, we'd deepened an already amazing friendship.

We decided to explore a few of the shops along River Street. It felt strange, but for once, we didn't have a timetable and there were no directions to follow. We passed bars and boutiques and T-shirt shops. In front of a coffee shop a young woman was handing out sample menus for a restaurant called Vic's on the River.

We each took a menu, to be polite more than anything else, while she explained that Vic's occupied the second, third, fourth, and fifth floors of the building behind her.

"The coffee shop is on River Street. The main entrance to Vic's is upstairs on Bay Street. But you don't have to walk all the way around. You can take the elevator up to the bar and dining room."

The menu was tempting, but it was just past 5:00, too early to eat. We probably would have continued on our way if she hadn't said one more thing.

"General Sherman's officers stayed here and in our main dining room, there's a map they drew on the wall showing the March to the Sea."

That was all we needed to hear. After a quick consultation with Milam, I asked the young woman, "Could we get a reservation for 7:00?"

She made a quick call, spoke and listened, then turned back to us. "They say they could seat you now. The earliest thing after that is 8:30."

8:30 was much too late, considering we had an early start planned for the next day.

"Guess not," Milam said.

The young woman smiled. "Well, you can still go up and see the map." She gestured behind her. "Just go through the shop and take the elevator up to the fourth floor. Maybe you can have a drink in the bar, too."

"We really should see it," Milam said.

So we walked down the little hall and got into the elevator. I pushed the button for 4, but before the doors closed a friendly, smiling man got on with us. By the time the doors opened on the fourth floor, we'd all introduced ourselves. He was Bill Hall, who, along with Dr. Irvin Victor, owned Vic's on the River, and he was gracious enough to show us around the place.

It was a lovely restaurant and the map lived up to its description. Bill explained that the hand-drawn map detailing Sherman's march from Tennessee through Georgia had been plastered over after the Civil War. But when the building was renovated in 1901, the map was discovered as the plaster was being removed. They were able to save a sizable fragment of the map. It now hangs in the main dining room behind a piece of protective plastic.

Bill allowed us to take his picture in front of the map. Unfortunately the reflections on the plastic covering prevented us from getting a good shot of the map itself. Next he took us out onto one of the balconies for what he said was the best view in the city of the Savannah River. It was, indeed, a glorious view.

Early or not, Milam and I asked if they could still seat us for dinner. How could we not dine there after such a hospitable welcome? Bill turned us over to his staff and we were immediately led to a table only a few feet from the famous map. Milam ordered wine. I had a martini. We both leaned back in our chairs, at peace with our world.

We'd already decided that this last night on the road was a time to splurge. Our research was done and we had a lot to celebrate. We ate well—pecan-crusted flounder for Milam and a filet with a Madeira demi-glace for me—and reminisced about some of the places we'd gone, people we met and the nearly magical things that had happened along the way.

Our meal became even more special when we learned that our server Amelia Thompson was a graduate of Mercer University—the home of our publisher Mercer Press. Like the Southerners we all were, Amelia, Milam, and I spent a little time comparing Mercer acquaintances to find the few we had in common. Satisfied with the connections we'd established, we went back to our meal and Amelia went to see to her other customers.

We ordered coffee, lingering longer than usual over the meal, then made our leisurely way back toward the hotel. People still filled the streets, but their movements were slower and their voices not so loud.

"We'll come back to Savannah," Milam said. "Maybe we can have a book signing down here."

"Definitely," I agreed. "All we have to do now is write the book."

Factors Row

Bill Hall, Vic's on the River

# Index